BEST

An Intimate Biography

WITHDRAWN

N.F.

WITHDRAWN

Other books by Michael Parkinson
(Published by Stanley Paul)

Football Daft
Cricket Mad
Sporting Fever

BEST

AN INTIMATE BIOGRAPHY

Michael Parkinson

Hutchinson of London

B . RES

The publishers acknowledge the following for permission to reproduce copyright photographs:

Colorsport / Dick Green / Ray Green / Keystone Press / Press Association / Syndication International

Hutchinson & Co (Publishers) Ltd
3 Fitzroy Square, London W1

London Melbourne Sydney Auckland
Wellington Johannesburg Cape Town
and agencies throughout the world

First published 1975
© Michael Parkinson Enterprises 1975

Set in Monotype Imprint
Printed in Great Britain by The Anchor Press Ltd
and bound by Wm Brendon & Son Ltd
both of Tiptree, Essex

ISBN 0 09 123420 4

2

To the man who inherits the crown

PROLOGUE

Dick Best is a small, benevolent, tubby man with a face as smooth and unlined as a polished horse brass. By comparison Anne Elizabeth Best's face reflects the struggle and the worry so commonplace among working-class women who have known nothing in their lives other than rearing children, washing, darning, cleaning, working part time to help out and wondering where the next penny is coming from. When she married in 1945 she was a pretty girl, and an outstanding athlete, having played for her country at hockey. Dick Best worked at a Belfast shipyard and eventually they set up home in a huge council estate on the outskirts of Belfast called the Cregagh. They didn't plan a family, it just happened. On 22 May 1946 at Belfast Royal Maternity Hospital Anne had a child. A boy. People with theories about genes will be interested to know that Anne Best is of pure Irish stock but Dick Best's family were immigrants from Scotland. Children of this pedigree often make great poets, marvellous soccer players and excellent boozers. They are also pretty good at self-destruction. The Bests called their boy George.

*   *   *

To say that Sir Matt Busby is mad about football is to insult him by understating the case. No man ever loved a game more, no man ever gained more from it nor suffered more cruelly because of it. Busby was, and is, a rare man in the world of soccer in that he has vision and imagination. In the late 1950s, in spite of typically insular and negative advice from the Football League management committee, he persuaded his directors to let him enter his team – Manchester United – in the European Cup competition. Busby saw clearly that soccer was becoming increasingly a world com-

7

petition and that in future the real prestige and the real riches lay in playing teams from overseas. He had built a team fit to compete with any club side in the world, and it mirrored Busby's delight in skilful, entertaining football and his genius for discovering young players.

Busby was one of the first British managers to realize that football is a young man's game. His simple adage was: 'If they are good enough, they are old enough'. The one player who so brilliantly sustained Busby's theory was Duncan Edwards. He played his first game for Manchester United at the age of fifteen years and eight months in 1953. Two years later he became the youngest player ever to win an England cap. Busby once said of him: 'I used to watch Duncan play and I knew why I loved the game so. The greatest, most fulfilling joy a manager can have is that of seeing a young boy arrive unknown, step on the field of play and then realise you have seen a great star make his début.'

Busby built his team around Edwards' massive and precocious talent. The first year they entered the European Cup they reached the semi-final, the next year, they again reached the semi-final.

To do so they had to visit Belgrade to play Red Star. They drew 3–3 and were through to the semi-final with a 5–4 aggregate. They flew home on 6 February in BEA Elizabethan G–ALZU A817 via Munich. At 15.03 the plane prepared for take off from Munich after two false starts. It never left the ground, crashing through the perimeter fence at 105 mph and hitting an unoccupied house 250 yards away. The undercarriage and the tail were torn off and a great team had been destroyed.

Seven players died immediately, the eighth, Duncan Edwards, fought his terrible injuries for two weeks, then he too died. Busby survived. Twice he was given the last rites, but he pulled through. He went back to Manchester and he rebuilt his team. His ambition remained the same: to win the European Cup. The dream he nurtured privately was that one day he might find another player to match Duncan Edwards. The ambition he knew to be possible, the dream he believed was hopeless but harmless.

In February 1961 he took a fifteen-year-old Belfast boy on to his playing staff, and although he didn't know it at the time, by doing so he achieved his ambition and fulfilled his dream. The boy's name was George Best and from the moment he signed for United nothing was the same again, not for Sir Matt, nor the club, and most certainly not for George Best.

CHAPTER 1

In the structure of a soccer club the talent scouts are the secret agents. They operate by stealth, pursuing a rumour here, checking a whisper there, in an increasingly competitive search for new talent. Good young soccer players are goal dust to the clubs. The cost of signing a young player, including a bonus to the scout and perhaps a sweetener here and there (strictly illegal, of course) is a blissful alternative to buying in the transfer market where nowadays ordinary players are costing £100000 or more and good players are simply priceless. Every scout's job is to find the new material and to persuade the boy and his parents that their particular club is the one to look after Sonny Jim's future.

Boys with talent are watched from the very first burgeoning of their talent. Malcolm Allison, manager of Crystal Palace, once had a report on a nine-year-old boy, watched him, was convinced of his skill and some years later when the child was old enough, signed him for Manchester City where Allison was manager at the time.

Competition for these youngsters is fierce and although inducements of any kind by the clubs are strictly illegal there is no doubt that they are sometimes made. It is difficult to obtain proof but some time ago while researching a programme on this subject for television I came across a man and his wife in the north of England whose son had recently signed for a leading club. The boy had a bright academic career ahead of him but chose instead to sign terms with a football club and I wondered why.

The father, who was a lorry driver, told me that they had been visited first by the scout of a club who told the parents he thought the boy had the talent to make a good player. On being told that he wasn't the first scout to have said that he immediately arranged an interview between the parents and the manager of the club he represented. Some time later the manager and his scout arrived and spent the evening trying to persuade the boy and his parents to join the club. The parents were still undecided when the couple left.

Later that evening while tidying up the room the wife found a paper parcel under the cushions of the chair where the manager had been sitting. She opened it and found £2000 in five-pound notes. The next day the husband rang the club and told the manager what he had found. 'It's not mine,' said the manager, 'I'd keep it if I were you.' The boy signed for the club.

It doesn't happen like that all the time, indeed the majority of signings are more or less above board, but it occasionally happens and it gives some idea of the kind of competition the club scout is involved in. The scout has one further problem and it is a fundamental and important one. How can you be sure that a boy of thirteen or fourteen is going to make the grade? The answer is, you can't. The precocious talent of the early teens can fade in later years, the overpowering strength of a well built teenager playing against smaller teenagers counts for naught against the big men in league football.

Some scouts recommend everything and everyone and seem to care little about the casualties. Some are cautious men whom the clubs rarely hear from. But when they do they know the recommendation will be sound. Such a man is Bob Bishop, Manchester United's scout in Northern Ireland. He is a quiet, anonymous man who quietly combs his way through Ireland looking for promising young players. He also runs a boys' team in Belfast called Boyland. One day in 1961 his under 17s played the Cregagh Boys' Club and lost 4–2. Bishop's team was destroyed by a young fifteen-year-old with the physique of a tooth-pick and the pallor of a child raised on chip butties. Bob Bishop contacted Matt Busby. He didn't waste words. 'I think I've found a genius,' he said.

*   *   *

GEORGE'S STORY

When they sent me to the psychiatrist after I'd run away for the first time – or was it the second – I can't remember, he started asking me all about my childhood as if he expected me to be illegitimate or daft or both. That psychiatrist asked dafter bloody questions than some journalists I know and that's saying something. 'Look,' I wanted to tell him, 'nobody put his hand up my trousers in the school bus nor was I raped by my favourite auntie. If I've fucked it up I've done it myself and what is more, I've enjoyed it!' That's what I wanted to say but I didn't. I just looked at him and said nothing. Like I used to do when Matt had a go at me. Yes, boss, no, boss. Bollocks.

I think I was a perfectly normal child. I was a bit lonely perhaps. Mum and Dad were both working and I used to spend a lot of time with my grandparents. There was one grandad, grandad Withers he was called, whom I was particularly fond of. He died the day I took my eleven plus and the family kept it from me. Thought it might ruin my chances of becoming a brain surgeon. I went in the shop that day on my way to school and the woman said, 'When's grandad getting buried?' and I thought she said, 'When's grandad getting married?' and I thought, silly cow, he's bloody married already.

Anyhow I got home and they told me he had died and I went out and sat under the street lamp and cried for two hours.

I passed the eleven plus, fat lot of bloody good that did me. I went to grammar school and hated it. They didn't play soccer and that's all I wanted to do. I started playing truant. I'd hide in the toilets at lunchtime and then go and play soccer in the afternoon. I used to play by myself using just a tennis ball. I never went anywhere without that bloody ball I knew even then I had talent as a soccer player and that's what I wanted to be. Sometimes I'd go shoplifting for a change. Nothing serious. Just a few pens and rulers from Woolies. I think I sometimes wanted to get caught because I wanted people to notice me.

I used to fake illness. I'd buy some wine gums and suck all the red ones until my throat was stained and then I'd go home and pretend to be dying from tonsillitis. So they sent me to bloody hospital and took them out. That's the trouble with being a good actor. But I fell in love for the first time in hospital. She was called Nurse Anderson, and she was the first, but not the last.

They kicked me out of grammar school, thank Christ, and I went to a secondary school where they played soccer. I played all day and all night and I knew I was good. I could do things the others couldn't even think about, never mind manage.

I joined a boys' club, the Cregagh, and we had a manager called Bud MacFarlane. He used to tell me that I was one of the best players he had seen and that I ought to think about making it a career. He used to write to Irish clubs about me and they'd send their scouts down but all of them said I was too small. Mind you they had a point. I looked like a stick of rhubarb. I weighed about seven stones and I was as thin as a matchstick.

I was very unattractive and I remember the birds teasing me. They used to shout 'Look at the skinny, ugly sod' when I walked past them. I used to want to grab them and thump them because it was true. Instead I put birds out of my mind. I didn't bother with them. You could say I made up for it later. When I wasn't playing I used to watch. My dad used to take me to a local soccer tournament called the Chicken Run held in the local dust bowl. Twenty-seven games in a day and the local St John Ambulance Brigade were the busiest people on the field. They had some players there who made Norman Hunter look normal.

My hero was a guy called Sticky Sloane and one of the best moments of my life was some time later when I'd made it with United. I was back home having a drink in a pub when this guy comes up to me and says, 'Could I have your autograph?' I looked at him and said, 'If I can have yours.' I meant it. It was Sticky Sloane. He nearly bloody fainted.

People always ask me where I got my skill from and they look disappointed when I say I don't know. But I don't. I'm lucky, I'm gifted. I've never had to think about the game or theorize about it. I hate being told what to do. I always did. Football's a simple game. The only advice I ever accepted was from Bud MacFarlane. One day he said to me, 'George, you are a bit weak on your left foot.' So all that week I practised with the tennis ball and my left foot. At nights I used to practise under the street lamps. The next Saturday I played with a plimsoll on my right foot and a boot on my left. I never touched the ball with my right foot and we won 21–0. I scored twelve, all with my left foot. People think I'm naturally left-footed. I'm just naturally gifted. I got better as I got older, but I didn't bloody grow any. I used to fantasize about walking down a tunnel on to a field with 60000 people calling my name. I didn't know where the ground was but I was playing for Wolves. I always fancied them.

It used to make me upset when I saw the scouts on the touchline and I'd play brilliantly and they'd just shake their heads and Bud would tell me later they'd say, 'Which refugee camp did you find him in?' There used to be a director of Glentoran football club who lived on our estate. He had a house right next to our soccer field and I used to pray before every game that one day he'd spot me and whisk me away to play for his team. He never showed.

I was fifteen and feeling rejected. I'd just about given up any thoughts of being a soccer player. Dad suggested that I get a job as an apprentice printer when I left school. I agreed. I'd have said yes to anything because if I couldn't play soccer it didn't matter what I did and I'd be bored stiff in any case. I wasn't cut out to be anything in particular except a footballer. My talent gave me that, my physique fitted me for apprentice dwarf in a circus.

One day I was playing and I saw this guy on the touchline. An ordinary guy wearing an open-necked shirt and a cloth cap. I asked Bud who he was. He said he was called Bob Bishop and he was a scout. I met him later at our house. He told me Manchester United wanted me to go for two weeks' trial. That night I ran down our street to the soccer pitch. The girls shouted, 'Where you going to, long streak of piss?'

'I'm off to play for Manchester United,' I shouted back.

'He's gone bloody mad,' they said.

I nearly did – but it took a while.

CHAPTER 2

George Best sailed for England on a hot July day in 1961. Two days later he returned home, fed up and homesick. The journey to Manchester had been a traumatic experience for a shy, slight lad from Belfast. There was confusion at the station about a taxi. The club sent one, Best missed it, hailed another, asked for Old Trafford and ended up at the cricket ground. When he finally arrived at the football ground he was rebuked by Joe Armstrong, the club's chief scout, for being late.

Best, who had, and still has, a pathological hatred of being bawled out, resented it.

He was taken to his digs, a semi-detached in the Manchester suburb of Chorlton, owned by a widow, Mrs Mary Fullaway. It was the only good thing to happen to him on that day. Twelve years later he still lives with Mrs Fullaway, a testament to his affection for her and a tribute to her stoicism in the face of the worry and despair her lodger has brought her.

She remembers when she first saw him: 'I wanted to sit him down and fill him full of meat and potatoes. He was so thin and tiny. He looked more like an apprentice jockey than a footballer.' Mary Fullaway is used to having footballers as lodgers. She is one of the landladies approved of by the club to look after their young apprentice players to see they eat the right food and go to bed on time. They are more than landladies, they become substitute mothers. Mary Fullaway had seen them come and she'd seen them go. She reckoned she knew a thing or two about soccer players and she didn't give George Best even a slender hope of succeeding.

The next day he went to the ground, saw some of the senior squad and believed himself that he didn't have a hope in hell. He went back to his digs, packed his bag and went back to Ireland.

Dick Best took his return philosophically. His son would be a printer. Matt Busby, however, was less fatalistic. He rang Dick Best and asked him to send George back. He had not seen the boy play but Bob Bishop's recommendation was mouth-watering and he felt sure that George had the talent to make a career as a professional player. Reluctantly Best returned.

He says now, 'I still hated it. I was homesick, miserable. I felt so bloody ignorant, so terribly puny. God knows what kept me there. It certainly wasn't the money.' Indeed his first wage packet contained £1 to help him with fares and meals throughout the week, because Best was still an amateur and the club was not allowed to sign him until he was seventeen. Equally the club was free to kick him out when he was seventeen so he was continually on trial.

Until it made up its mind about Best the club found him work near the ground. He was expected to graft for a firm during the day and train at night. He wanted to train all day. The club wouldn't allow it. George Best was sent to work as a messenger boy at the Manchester Ship Canal Company's office. He left. They sent him as an invoice clerk to the offices of another shipping company. He left. They fixed him up with a job at a timber yard. He left after three hours. The club began to tumble the fact that Master Best had a mind of his own.

Wisely they found him a job at an electrical firm where he had only to work afternoons and could train every morning. It was the first time Best had come into conflict with the club and in retrospect the incident takes on a new significance. Best worked his way slowly through the youth sides becoming physically and mentally more adapted to life at Old Trafford. He little realized the stir he was causing in the club.

When Best arrived in 1961 United were in trouble. They finished fifteenth in the table, their lowest position for a long time.

This was the year that Tottenham Hotspur won the double and were the last great and entertaining club side produced in England. The Spurs side had all the talents in proper balance. The cool intelligence of Blanchflower in partnership with the rugged technique of Dave Mackay. The provider and the destroyer. In the forward line the thunder of Bobby Smith flourished alongside the genius of Jimmy Greaves. The battering ram and the sniper. Add to that the skills of John White, one of the greatest of the modern inside-forwards, and you have a team fit to set alongside any of the great club sides, of any time.

As I say, it was the last great and entertaining side we produced because soccer changed in the sixties. The dreamers departed and men of pragmatic character took over. United stood for a while against change and, as we shall see, with the help of Best's skill managed to bring some beauty and entertainment into the game, but they were never, in my view, a great side. Good but not great. Liverpool and Leeds who demand recognition for their successes during the sixties and seventies similarly cannot be compared with the Spurs side, being too functional, too obsessed with tactics and theory to ever be called entertaining.

In 1961 Busby looked with envy at Tottenham Hotspur. They were his kind of team, playing the game where it should be played, on the ground. He had built two great teams and he was determined to do so again. He went into the transfer market. Shortly after Spurs had beaten United 3—1 in the semi-final of the Cup he heard that Denis Law, playing for Torino in the Italian league, had been taken off the field by his manager for allegedly not trying. On 12 July 1962, Busby signed him for £115 000. He spent nearly £200 000 more on other players but in the season 1962–3 the team was, for a while, in danger of relegation.

In February of '63 Busby bought a wing-half from Celtic called Paddy Crerand, a mature, intelligent player, a marvellous passer of a ball. In spite of its awful League position the club did well in the Cup, getting to Wembley and beating Leicester 3—1. Law scored two goals and Crerand had a remarkable game, spraying the park with long and perceptive passes, dictating the game as his whims and fancy took him. Matt Busby started to scent the beginnings of a good team. He had extraordinary players like Law, Crerand and Bobby Charlton. But he needed one more ingredient, the player like Big Duncan who could do the lot.

In other words, the perfect player.

Pat Crerand believed he had already seen one. Shortly after

18

arriving at Old Trafford he went to see one of United's youth teams play. Being a Scotsman reared on the true tradition of skill and ball play Crerand can get rapturous when talking about good players. His lecture on George Best can take up to two hours or more depending on his mood and it had its beginnings that day in '63 when he sat next to trainer Jack Crompton to pass a few moments watching some young kids kick a ball about.

'I wasn't going to stay very long and then all of a sudden this kid on the park starts playing like a mixture of di Stefano and Denis Law. I'd never seen anything like it. He's hitting long balls with both feet that are carving the defence, the full-back's got legs like bloody corkscrews he's turning him so much and he's whacking the ball past the keeper from all angles. I turned to Jack Crompton. "By God, Jack," I said, "that boy is some player."

' "Yes, we think he might be," said Jack.

'Might be! Jesus, you could have sold your house and put the proceeds on that boy becoming one of the great players in the world. There was nothing to stop him – except himself.'

One or two United players who had been at the club before Crerand arrived were equally convinced of Best's remarkable ability. One of them was Harry Gregg, the Irish international goalkeeper, a survivor of the Munich air crash, now manager of Swansea Town. Gregg, like Best, was from Northern Ireland and in the awkward early days went out of his way to help the apprentice settle down. It meant a lot to Best who to this day retains a real affection for Gregg.

'He was like a god to me. When I first met him he was one of the best goalies in Britain, an Irish international, good looking, sweet talking. Everything I wasn't and everything I hoped to be. I couldn't believe it when he spoke to me and generally tried to make me feel at home. I've always been friendly with him – even when I started going off the rails he was one of the few who never rubbished me, always ready to up and say, "Come on, kid, what's the matter? Can I help?" '

Indeed in Best's penultimate crisis with the club, after he had been put on the transfer list, Gregg tried to persuade Best to join

19

him at Swansea, then in the fourth division. The idea of Best play-ing in fourth division football was treated as a ludicrous joke by the *cognoscenti*. It is a mark of his respect for Gregg that Best gave the proposition serious thought.

The growing affection between the man and the young boy was threatened only once in the formative stages. In his playing days Gregg was renowned as a fierce competitor. He literally hated people scoring goals against him and had been known to pursue rejoicing opponents to the half-way line threatening dire conse-quences if they dare put another past him that afternoon. Best, on the other hand, is a player who delights in making a mockery out of opponents, particularly dirty players and goalkeepers. In his first training session with the first-team squad when he was about sixteen and still unknown, Best decided to play a joke on Harry Gregg. The first time he received the ball he sent Gregg the wrong way, diving after an imaginary ball, while he pushed the real one firmly into the opposite corner of the net. Gregg took it as a fluke and so did the rest of the first-team squad. But after it happened twice more they began to get the message. The players thought it a huge joke. Gregg says, 'If I could have caught him, I'd have bloody murdered him'.

It was during sessions like this that Best revealed a rare and awesome talent. Paddy Crerand said, 'We used to have a saying when George got the ball in practice games. As soon as he got possession I'd shout, "Let's have another ball on the park for the rest of us to play with". You couldn't get him to part with the bloody thing.'

He was seventeen, eight and a half stone and improving all the time, when Busby signed him as a professional for £25 a week. The question now was when should he put him into the first team. Busby never doubted his ability. When Best arrived at the club Matt took a look at him and told his staff, 'Let him alone. Don't try and coach him. The boy is special.' The only question mark was against his physique and his courage. The first division was no place for slender young men who delighted in taking the mickey out of opponents. Such fripperies were likely to earn the perpetrator a bed in the nearest casualty ward.

'If they are good enough, they are old enough.' The old adage. It worked for Big Duncan. Yes, but Duncan was a man at fourteen with legs like young oaks and a physique and temperament only the foolish or the very brave would mess with.

This boy Best was still frail. They'd break him in two. In the end Busby backed his principles. He'd always believed that skill and talent not strength were the fundamentals of good soccer.

Four months after signing Best on his seventeenth birthday, Busby picked him to play against West Bromwich Albion. Busby knew he was launching a star. What he couldn't know was that he was giving the stage to a young man who was to become one of the most exciting footballers the world has ever seen, someone who would be a cult figure for millions of people. George Best was to become a star of international proportions. The fifth Beatle. He was also heading towards a spectacular disaster.

*   *   *

GEORGE'S STORY

In those days when I was a kid the only thing I shared my bed with was a football. I used to take a ball to bed with me. I know it sounds daft but I used to love the feel of it. I used to hold it, look at it and think, 'One day you'll do everything I tell you'. I only lived to play football. I hated all the bloody jobs they made me do when I was an apprentice. I hate people bossing me about, and the work was so boring. When I was at work or supposed to be working, I'd fantazise about games I was going to play in. It was always at Wembley and there were 100000 people in the ground and it was a Cup Final. I turned on the most incredible bloody show anyone had ever seen in a football ground.

First I'd take a ball on my thigh and bounce it in the air as I ran the length of the field. I actually did it once in a game against West Ham and all I got was a bollocking from Denis Law. Then I'd trap the ball by sitting on it. You know, there'd be a long clearance downfield and I'd control it with my arse. Then we'd be awarded a penalty and I'd walk up to the keeper, point to the underside of the crossbar and say, 'It's going in off there'. And it would. The other variation on the penalty routine was to do a quick double shuffle in front of the ball so that I actually tapped it with my left foot then whacked it with my right but so quick that neither the keeper nor the ref would be sure if I'd kicked it twice or not.

I know they sound daft but I've done them all in training or in a game sometimes. I love taking the piss out of players too. Like 'nutmegging' them. That's sticking it between their legs and running round them. When I first started I didn't mind the hard men too much because it gave me the chance to rubbish them with my skill. I'd go past them and they'd say, 'Do that again and I'll break your fucking leg!' And next time I'd do 'em again and they'd say, 'Right, I fucking warned you'. Next time I got the ball I'd stand on it and beckon them to me. I used to be like a bullfighter, taunting them, inviting them to charge me. They rarely got me. I was too quick. At moments like that, with the crowd cheering I used to get the horn. Honestly. It used to arouse me, excite me.

I felt the same way every time I walked on to the field at the start of a game. I've seen other players be sick before they went out. Most are nervous. They hear the crowd outside chanting and shouting and they start shitting themselves. But it used to make me happy. The first time I played for the first team Matt made me twelfth man for a game at home against West Bromwich. He always intended playing me but he didn't want me to have a sleepless night on Friday so he sent me to bed thinking I'd just be the reserve. I didn't know that and what he didn't know was that instead of going to bed for a kip I spent the night wishing someone would fall downstairs and break a bloody leg or something so I could get in the team.

When he told me next day I was playing I felt calm and confident. There were 50000 in the ground that Saturday and when I got in the tunnel and heard them I knew this was where I belonged. I played on the wing and was marked by Graham Williams. In the dressing room the lads had joked about him being a cruncher and how he was going to have me for breakfast. Well, he's no cream puff. He whacked me in the first half and I changed wings in the second half but I enjoyed it. That Graham Williams was a character. I played against him a lot and a year after I first played against him he said to me, 'Stand still for a minute and let me see your face'. I thought he'd gone mental.

'Why?' I said.

'Well,' he said, 'I'm curious to know what you look like. I've played against you a lot and all I've seen is your backside disappearing up the touchline.'

After that first game I knew I'd arrived. I knew then what I'd always believed, that I'd find it easy to play in the first division. It sounds bloody arrogant but it's not. I always knew I had a great gift because I always found soccer a simple game to play. I'd seen other players, good ones, struggling to learn skills that I had naturally.

It used to annoy me when people thought something I did was a fluke. I remember once playing against Ipswich and I scored direct from a corner. Now I used to practise that. I used to be able to stick them in the net direct from the corner spot nine times out of ten. This time against Ipswich I tried it and it worked beautifully just inside the angle where I wanted it to go. Next day in the bloody press they're saying it was a lucky bloody goal. It made me so bloody mad that I wanted to write to them and explain. Anyway about two weeks later we're playing them in the Cup and in the first five minutes we got a corner. I took it and thought, 'I'll show you another bloody fluke'. It just missed. It scraped the angle on the wrong side. If it had gone in I was going to walk up to the press box, bow and walk off the field, Mr George Best, entertainer extraordinary, has made his point and will now retire. Looking back I had so much fun. Sometimes I sit and think where it really all went wrong.

CHAPTER 3

Best's entry into first division football was quiet, noticed only by a few observers.

David Meek, a sports writer with the *Manchester Evening News*, who has followed Manchester United for about eighteen years, reported Best's first game thus:

'There was the prospect of young George Best to brighten a dullish match. Despite the ordeal of a League début after only three reserve matches, a gruelling duel with full-back Graham Williams, and a painful ankle injury, he played pluckily and finished the game in style. None of the handicaps could disguise a natural talent. I know manager Matt Busby is looking forward to seeing this Belfast boy in a team with Law to help him. I agree, and it is an exciting prospect that will brighten up even the dullest of games.'

Busby took a more cautious point of view and left him out of the first team until Christmas when he recalled Best who scored his first League goal against Burnley and played out the rest of the season. In that time he had a taste of European football, being in the side that lost to Sporting Lisbon in the quarter final of the European Cup Winners Cup. Also in April 1964, after only twenty-one first-team games, Ireland gave him his first international cap. Manchester United finished runners-up in the Football League. It was an impressive start but what followed was startling. In the next season, his first full season in League football, Best showed all his remarkable talent as an athlete. In the record books the season is significant because United won the League and Denis Law scored twenty-eight goals, but to anyone following that season as I did the event of real relevance was the form of George Best. In his first games with United the season before, there were indications of things to come but I always felt that Best was holding himself on a tight rein, nervous perhaps of showing off in such illustrious company. Or perhaps it was that he could not believe he would find playing in the first division as easy as he did. In any event from the very beginning of the season 1964-5 he played with a confidence that was startling in one so young and revealed a staggering variety of skills sufficient to make the most discriminating connoisseur drool at the very mention of his name.

To understand Best's impact on the game one has to consider the state of British soccer in the mid sixties. For some time managers had been turning their backs on players with ball skills and individual talents and concentrating instead on hard-running, all-purpose players. Alf Ramsey, later to be knighted for his services to football, was patiently building a national team of admittedly incredible efficiency but one with an equally incredible ability to bore the pants off all but the most chauvinistic soccer supporter. Ramsey's team won the World Cup in 1966 mainly, I believe, because it played all its games at Wembley and also because in a crucial game against Argentine the South Americans committed suicide by being unable to control their unpredictable temperaments.

The point is, Ramsey's robots won the World Cup and British soccer managers, not renowned for their individuality, slavishly followed his pattern of creating teams in which stamina counted for more than skill and mediocrity, given a willing heart and strong legs, was rewarded while more artistic but less muscular attributes were rejected.

As I say, the pattern had been designed some time before 1966. Our winning the World Cup merely gave it the seal of approval. As early as 1960 Matt Busby wrote:

'Without wishing to belittle the achievements of any club I believe certain methods of attaining success have influenced British football too much and in the wrong direction. I am thinking of the power game. Results are achieved by placing too much emphasis on speed, power and physical fitness. Such teams now have many imitators. We are breeding a number of teams whose outlook seems to be that pace, punch and fitness are all that is required to win all the honours in the game. They forget that without pure skills

25

these virtues count for precisely nothing. I should like to see the honours in England won by a pure footballing side, the sort of team that concentrates on ball skills above all else.'

Busby's was not altogether a voice in the wilderness. The great Spurs side built entirely on these skills won the double. It was, as I said before, the last great and entertaining club side to be built in Britain. The rest settled for the 'power game', an apt description except that it suggests an excitement which its exponents most certainly did not project. Moreover it became a useful euphemism for another poisonous root which began to flourish in the sixties, the tactic of cancelling out skill with brutality.

Football is a game of physical contact and it had always had its fair share of tough and dirty players whose attributes implied that they slept nights in steel cages and lived on raw meat. Most teams had one such player, beloved of the home fans, hated by the opposition and carefully watched by the referees. The difference during the sixties was that in most teams every player could do a bit. The majority of professional footballers became destroyers, not creators, adept at preventing the other team playing by fair means or foul. The all-purpose, clockwork player could run all day, harrying and niggling at opponents, preventing them settling into any constructive system or pattern. The days of the thoughtful, cultured inside-forward who could settle on the ball, dictate the ebb and flow of the game with his creative instincts were long gone. To dwell on the ball for a split second was to get kicked in the air by an opponent who had no time for such delicate niceties.

Wing men, once the star turn of soccer, the magicians who dribbled down the touchline, the ball seemingly attached to their feet by elastic, became redundant, and were replaced by overlapping defenders who didn't know how to beat opponents, had not the slightest idea how to cross a ball and were to the real thing as clog dancing is to classical ballet. Centre-forwards, the glamour boys of the game, the goal scorers, became 'strikers' or 'target men'. The nomenclature was colourful but another deception. Whereas centre-forwards were the executioners of a grand design, 'strikers' found themselves the victims of another design more cynical than grand. The new concept of the game left them lonely, valiant figures in the opposition penalty area surrounded by defenders who made goal scoring a difficult and painful business. To operate up front called for the kind of blind courage displayed by bomb disposal experts or kamikaze pilots.

Thus football in the sixties was dominated by the simple and somewhat cynical theory that it is easier to stop people playing than to encourage people who can play. At the same time, and paradoxically considering the tripe that was being served up by the majority of clubs, soccer was building up towards a newfound prosperity. England's World Cup success in 1966, a celebration of mediocrity rivalled only by our joy at winning the Eurovision song contest, brought a new and mainly undiscerning audience to football. It was to last until the people proved that they couldn't be fooled all of the time and began staying away from soccer grounds in their thousands. But while it lasted it created a whole new industry in which even moderate soccer players were elevated to star status and slender talents rewarded with excessive salaries.

A few years before George Best first played for Manchester United the soccer player had been little more than a downtrodden slave, a menial servant paid £20 a week and not a penny more because of a ruling fixing a maximum rate for a soccer player. This iniquitous state of affairs was broken by a vigorous and brash young player called Jimmy Hill who, as leader of the Professional Footballers Association, conducted a brilliant campaign for the abolition of the maximum wage and won. This opened the way towards new horizons for the player. Soon Johnny Haynes of Fulham became the first footballer to earn £100 a week.

Once upon a time a professional soccer player was indistinguishable from the fan behind the goal. Indeed in many cases the fan earned more than the player. They were stars in shabby macs whom you could meet in billiards halls. You could even find yourself sitting next to your hero on a bus. Their descendants in the sixties had altogether more swagger. They drove Jags and drank at more exclusive bars. Nothing flash, but middle class and quietly prosperous. For all that the real heroes, the Moores and the Charltons, exemplified the British idea of true sportsmen, cleancut, chivalrous, modest, sober, quiet-living family men. Soccer in the early sixties represented graft and hard work, a muscular idealism that had appeal but little glamour. George Best gave it glamour all right, and a lot else besides, some of which it had never bargained for.

*   *   *

GEORGE'S STORY

I wish I'd been born in Brazil. I really do! Things might have been different then. The way they play the game with the emphasis on ball control, skill and talent, is what it's all about. You watch the Brazilians in form and you can set it to music, can't you? I mean if you were sitting at home and it's fifty-fifty whether to watch the telly or go to a game, you're going to go a million miles to see players like Pele and Gerson. But say it's fifty-fifty and the top two clubs in the first division are playing in your backyard, you'd want your bloody head testing if you got out of your chair. The attitude to soccer in this country is all wrong. It's improved at international level since Alf went but it's still not right.

Basically I used to think of myself as an entertainer. It was my job to go out there and give them a show. I don't think the game is worth playing unless you enjoy it because if the player enjoys it there's got to be a chance the spectators will like it too. The game today is so bloody dreary, isn't it? No colour, no excitement. All that bollocks about zonal defence and 4–4–2 and all that crap. We were never a great side at United but there was a spell when we were a bloody good one and that was when we played it off the cuff with five forwards attacking and two wing half-backs who moved up with us. It wasn't bad when we had David Herd, Denis Law, Bobby Charlton, John Connelly and myself up front and Paddy creating things in midfield. Then, later on, when things started going wrong at my club we used to play two up front and bang high balls up to them just like any other club in the country. The point is, United is not just any other club, is it?

It amazed me we ever got it right at United because to me the training was a joke. Jack Crompton, the trainer, used to come out carrying these two balls under his arm and occasionally he'd let us have a kick but only after we'd knackered ourselves running up and down and round the pitch. Stamina's all right, you've got to be able to run, but you've also got to be able to do the main thing and the main thing at soccer is to know what to do with the ball.

At its simplest level that's what is wrong with British football today. Too many people who can run all day but can't kick a bloody football. The continentals and the South Americans are streets ahead of us when it comes to skill and that is what the game is all about. It's really a question of practice and emphasis. I used to stay behind at Old Trafford when training was officially over and practise things. I'd stand forty or fifty yards from goal and try and hit the crossbar, then stick 'em in the net from any angle. Just generally get to know the ball and how to master it.

Of course you can make a good argument that it is no good learning the skills nowadays because you're only going to get yourself kicked for your trouble. And it's true. I was one of those players who was marked down for what's called 'special attention'. This means that the nearest man kicks him.

English teams have the reputation for being the hardest but I doubt it. I'd rather play against an English team any day than an Italian or an Argentinian side. I think the difference is that we're not very good at it whereas they are masters at dirty play. In this country there's a reason for fouling a player, but the Italians and Argentinians don't need a reason. They just kick you because you're wearing a different shirt. They are very good at sticking their elbows in your throat, spitting, grabbing your balls as you wait for corner kicks, eye gouging and play acting.

We were playing once in a European Cup game at Old Trafford and I was brought down near their goal. The keeper comes out, bends down, says nice as pie, 'How are you?' Offers me his hand and then digs his nails into my skin. I let out a yell, swung a backhand at him and he goes down like he's been hit by a truck. He's a six foot ten fella so I know I'm in trouble. In situations like this I always used to look for Paddy Crerand. Paddy wasn't a dirty player, just the opposite, but he was a case-hardened Scots nut when it came to bother. He could look after himself and he used to look after me. I said, 'Paddy, that keeper's going to get me'.

29

Paddy says, 'Here at Old Trafford in front of our crowd and our lads? Don't be daft. He's got no chance.'

Anyhow the final whistle goes and I bolt for the tunnel and this bastard comes chasing after me. So I get alongside Paddy and I say, 'Excuse me, can I have a word with you?' At that moment the goalie grabs me and socks me. Paddy sticks him up against the tunnel wall and whacks him. He must have been a strong bastard because Paddy belts him straight on the chin and he just shakes his head and starts punching. The funny thing was that Matt came down to sort it all out, and was just about to open his mouth and appeal for peace and common sense when he got clocked too.

Our British players are quite civilized by comparison. They get called dirty bastards, stuffers, destroyers and the like but they never really bothered me because they weren't very efficient. Take Norman Hunter and Tommy Smith. They are hard men but they are not evil.

To my mind, that Peter Storey was a joke. How on earth did he get to play for England? I mean he couldn't even stop another player playing. My grandmother could do a better job. It's the easiest thing in the world to mark someone in a game. You can stop the best players if you stand in their boots. I used to say that if all I had to do in soccer was mark another player, I'd give the game up. And I meant it. These close markers used to really piss me off at times.

Once I signed a modelling contract for clothes and the company wanted some action shots of me to spread through the pages of the catalogue. I arranged for the photographer to come to Old Trafford when we were playing Chelsea. Some time later I saw the photographer and asked him if the shots were O.K. He looked dejected. 'Not really,' he said. I asked why. 'Well, I took over 300 shots of you throughout the game but in every picture there's a bullet-headed guy in a number six shirt standing next to you.' It was 'Chopper' Harris earning his money following me round the park.

Sometimes you hear 'Break his fucking leg!' from the opposition's bench but I don't think they mean it, and even if they did they don't have the experts to do the job properly. I mean you've got to be very good to break someone's leg.

The players I objected to most were the ones who rarely got a mention in anyone's list of hard men. The crafty men who did it quietly and efficiently. I'm not saying any of them ever tried to hurt anyone but they could be nasty and they'd get away with it week after week.

Some players used to get upset by the language on the field because there are footballers who never stop talking. I don't know how they've got breath left to play. They'd say to me, 'Try to pass me today and you've got no chance', or 'Our skipper's going to kill you, we told him you were fucking his wife last night', or 'Where's your bleeding handbag, you long-haired puff?' It used to make me laugh, but it upsets some players and, of course, some referees couldn't stand it.

Everyone f's and blinds on a football field. I mean it's impossible not to get keyed up and involved with 50 000 people screaming their heads off. But with some refs, as soon as they heard you say, 'Fuck me, ref', or something like that, you were booked. Others, like Gordon Hill, would give it back in spades. You'd say to Gordon, 'That was a stupid bloody decision', and he'd say, 'You're not playing too well either'. Next time you kept your mouth shut because he'd take the piss out of you.

I rate Gordon Hill. I think he's a fine referee and there's not many I'd say that about. Come to think about it after mentioning Gordon Hill I don't think there is another referee I'd care to comment on.

My language on the field was always a bit ripe. I used to call Denis Law a prick and he'd give it me back. I'd do the same to Bobby Charlton and he'd give as good as he got. The only difference being that I didn't mean what I said to Denis but in Bobby's case I was understating my feelings. I just couldn't get on with Bobby Charlton. When I first went to Old Trafford I thought he was a god. Later I couldn't stand the sight of him. In the last three years at Old Trafford we never spoke except to say, 'Good morning', if we were in a good mood.

He didn't like me either, that was fairly obvious. I think he felt I was letting the club down by my behaviour and maybe he was right, but it was none of his fucking business and in any case I carried that team for a couple of seasons and he never came up to me then and said, 'Well done, my son'. I couldn't stand his holier-than-thou attitude and that image of the fine upstanding athlete. I thought he was a bloody misery.

I also thought he was overrated as a player. He was a good player all right but not a great player like everyone said.

He was one of those players it was hard to criticize because the public loved him too much. He looked good on the ball, didn't he? But how many times did he hold it too long and break up the rhythm of our attack?

He never got the special treatment I got nor Denis Law got mainly because the other players daren't kick him because he was like a bloody national institution.

I used to do a lot of drinking in a pub in Manchester which had a picture of Bobby on the wall. It was a painting actually. One night, when I was feeling particularly fed up, I bought two dozen eggs and threw them at his bloody picture. Wallop! All over the bloody place.

That's what I thought about him.

Often people say to me, 'If only you'd had Bobby Charlton's temperament'.

I'd have lasted longer, that's for sure, but would life have been as sweet?

CHAPTER 4

There never was a boy more ideally equipped for his place in time. In the early sixties the Beatles created the first post-war generation with its own culture and real individual identity. Looking at Best's career in those first few years it is impossible not to regard him as the fifth Beatle. The very month in 1963 when the Beatles had their first hit, Best made his début with Manchester United. The Beatles defied all the conventions of pop music and created a new style. Best disregarded all the theories of modern football and showed us a different and altogether more exciting and beautiful game.

Like the Beatles he gave a sense of identity and purpose to the kids while appealing also to an older generation who liked his boyish impudence and his unconventional good looks. The Beatles created new fashion, so did Best. He grew his hair long, defying the convention that athletes had short-back-and-sides and anyone who didn't was a cissy. Other players followed suit. He grew a moustache and suddenly every player in Britain had a growth on his upper lip. He sported a beard and for the first time since Edwardian days soccer players stopped shaving. I have little doubt that had he taken the field wearing war paint the rest would have followed his example.

It would be wrong, however, to suggest that Best's influence on soccer happened immediately. It had quiet beginnings. In January 1965 Brian Glanville of *The Sunday Times* wrote:

George Best is a new wave star. Eighteen years old in a sober and discreet blue tailored suit, maroon handkerchief peeping from the pocket, maroon knitted tie. There are signs of exuberance in the cuffed sleeves on his jacket, the sheepdog abundance of his hair style . . . Whatever the cuffed shirts, the haircut ('I was late for a cup match; I combed it back and I scored twice. I liked it like that and I kept it'),

Best's modus vivendi is familiar, even traditional. It's true that when he says, 'I send quite a lot of money home, I usually only draw out £20 a week', one recollects that a few years ago £20 was the maximum wage. Yet even so, 'I've usually got plenty of it left over, but I put most of it in a building society.'

Again he's just bought an Austin 1100 but he still lives in digs, and 'goes to the pictures once or twice a week' or otherwise 'goes ten pin bowling'. Plus ça change. The new wave is coming in gently.

Glanville, while acknowledging Best's other contribution to the game saw his real significance as a player. He noted in the same article, 'this season he has been the terror of the first division full-backs, a tiny but determined figure with superb control and equilibrium, fine acceleration and the courage both to best bigger men and challenge them in circumstances where he might get hurt'.

Glanville immediately spotted Best's real importance to United, stating, 'For all Law's brilliance, all Charlton's moments of genius, Best is vital to them. He was vital to them in the floodlit match they won at Chelsea last September when he outshone everyone else on the pitch, ubiquitous and unstoppable, conjuring the ball away from defenders with magic dexterity.'

This was the game that Paddy Crerand rates as Best's most masterful display, the moment when Crerand knew for certain he was playing alongside one of the greatest players the game had seen.

It took place under floodlights on 20 September 1964, with United and Chelsea neck and neck at the top of the first division. Best was marked by Ken Shellito, a fine young full-back, who that evening suffered cruelly as Best beat him at will. George turned him so many ways, that, as Crerand observed with relish, 'Shellito was taken off suffering from twisted blood'.

Sir Matt says, 'It was one of the many great displays he gave at Chelsea. Something about the ground used to lift him, make him play better. But I shall always remember that first time. Ever after that when we went to Stamford Bridge I thought I ought to have phoned the police and told them a murder was about to be committed.'

That night in 1964 Best's play was a revelation. More than that, to fans parched of spectacle and wit, it came as a shower of refreshing rain in a drought. That night, as Arthur Hopcraft in his splendid book, *The Football Man*, observed, was one of the occasions when Best brought back the verb 'to dribble' to the sportswriter's vocabulary.

As Crerand says now, 'You could see in that game the complete range of his skills. That is what made him so special, his range. He could do more things better than any player I have ever seen. He was a magnificent distributor of a ball, he could beat a man on either side using methods that no one had ever thought about, he could shoot, he could tackle, he was competitive and yet cool under pressure.

'What more could you want? I mean what is the perfect player? Two good feet? The kid had them. Strong in the air? He could beat men twice his size. Ability to score goals? Only Greavsy and Law have equalled him and I think his ability to score a goal out of nothing was even greater than theirs. Courage? I've never seen a braver player. He could play at the back, in midfield or anywhere up front. He was probably the best bloody keeper at the club too, but we never tried him.'

Sir Matt assessed his skills thus, 'George Best was gifted with more individual ability than I have ever seen in any other player, certainly unique in the number of gifts. He remained deceptively skinny looking but he was strong and courageous to a degree that compensated amply. He had more ways of beating a player than any other player I have ever seen. Every aspect of ball control was perfectly natural to him from the start. He even used his opponents' shins to his advantage by hitting the ball on to them so accurately that it came back to him like a one-two pass.

'He had more confidence in his ability than I have ever seen in any other sportsman. He was always able to use either foot (sometimes he seemed to have six!) His heading was devastating. If he had a fault in those younger days it was that he wanted to beat too many opponents when he could have passed the ball to better advantage. You could see him beat two or three or even four and then lose the ball and you would be having apoplectic fits and saying to yourself, "Why the hell don't you pass the ball more?"

Then he would beat four men and score the winner. What do you do about that?'

The same question was often asked by opponents who found themselves spending a fruitless afternoon chasing after this extraordinary player. He posed them problems they had never even considered before. More often than not they countered skill with brute force but Best's unique balance enabled him to evade the most savage tackle and his remarkable speed of acceleration from a standing start took him clear of the scything tackle designed to bring him down to his opponents' speed and playing level.

In those days he played with a passionate commitment and total involvement. He eschewed the histrionics of lesser players, regarding any stoppage as an infringement on his time. When fouled in mid flight he displayed irritation only in the sense that someone had foiled his scheme and not, as happened later, because someone had had the temerity to kick him.

Often he took revenge spectacularly by teasing an opponent, 'nutmegging' him, making him look silly. But these were the only indulgences he allowed himself. Busby reckons that had he fallen in the penalty area as often as many players did and still do, he could have had a dozen penalties a year. But Best never took a dive. The one that brought him down had to be a good one because his pride wouldn't let him succumb to a bad one.

George Best, footballer, was on the way to being Georgie, superstar. In his first full season his team had won the first division championship and he was the most talked about player in British football.

In 1966 he went to Lisbon to play against Benfica and lit a bonfire against the killjoys who were destroying football. That night he inspired United to what can be argued was among their greatest performances as they beat one of the world's great club teams 5—1 in their own backyard. Geoffrey Green, of *The Times*, described United's performance as 'the most inspired, inspiring and controlled performance I have seen from any British side abroad in the past twenty years. Had I not seen it I would not have believed it.'

He described Best's performance thus: 'Best, with his long dark mop of hair, is known in these parts as "The Beatle". Now he was the best of all, as he set a new, almost unexplored, beat. He seemed quite suddenly to be in love with the ball and the whole side followed his lead.'

Remembering the game nowadays Sir Matt shakes his head, still dumbfounded by what his team did that night: 'I told them to play it tight for a while, for twenty minutes or so, until we got their measure. George just went out and destroyed them. I couldn't believe it and they most certainly couldn't until it was too late. They were also prepared to play it tight for a while. After all that is what always happened in European Cup games. Then out comes this kid as if he's never heard of tradition and starts running at them, turning them inside out. I ought to have shouted at him for not following instructions. But what can you say? He was a law unto himself. He always was.'

United didn't win the European Cup that year, but Busby knew now that he had the one player capable of carrying him to his ambition. There was one slight worry. That same season Matt had called Best into his office and told him he was dropped. Matt told the player he was mixing with the wrong crowd, forgetting about the game, staying out until all hours. George said he was sorry. Matt left him out for a couple of weeks and when he came back he was better than ever. Still there was a worry in Matt's mind, a niggling doubt.

Best appeared to have no reservations whatsoever about the future. The display at Lisbon made him an international star, gave him a larger canvas to fantasize upon. Coming back from Lisbon he bought a large sombrero. He stuck it on his head at London airport. The photographers were delighted. The *Daily Mirror* had him on front and back pages in the same issue. Surely some kind of a record.

Normally reticent men called him 'a genius'. The 'streak of piss' from Belfast started getting fan mail from girls who obviously thought him desirable.

A record company asked him to make a pop record.

Sir Matt said 'No' on George's behalf.

He opened a boutique, he acquired an agent.

Everyone told him, 'Get it all together, George, and you'll be a millionaire by the time you're thirty.'

Everyone envied George.

He had climbed his mountain without breaking sweat.

What nobody realized at the time was that the beginning, so successful and glamorous, was also the beginning of the end.

As Sir Matt replied when I asked him to put a date on Best's decline, 'From the moment he made it at the top,' he said.

Matt realized that too late.

So did George.

* * *

GEORGE'S STORY

I knew I was a good player and I knew I'd become well known but I wasn't prepared for what happened to me. It was like some bloody great roundabout with music playing and I couldn't get off. I liked it at first. I was flattered when I came out of the ground and people wanted my autograph. I noticed I got more birds waiting for me than the others, then I noticed that when I touched the ball on the field you could hear this shrill noise in the crowd with all the birds screaming like at a Beatles concert. It was this reaction to me that interested me most.

The reaction to my playing ability was good but no more than I expected. I mean they used to call me a 'genius' and all that. Well, it's a big word but I knew what they meant. I never doubted my ability on the field. I knew I had great gifts so I wasn't surprised when people remarked on them. Looking back those were the most enjoyable days. I didn't give a bugger. I made enough money to live without a care. I enjoyed every moment on a football field and I discovered women. Or they discovered me.

It was incredible. I never had to do any work, take them out for dinner or any of that crap. They'd ring me up or hang about in the boutique and straight upstairs. I had a flat above the shop. In fact I think the only reason I opened a boutique in the first place was because it had a flat above it and it was a great knocking shop. Also it was a cover from the boss and the club. They liked to think I was living a pure life in my digs. Well I was, but I was leading another kind of life in that flat and the boss would have gone grey if he'd known what was happening.

I suppose I was a bit daft from the start. It's not good for an athlete to spend every afternoon fucking, every evening drinking and every morning thinking about fucking and drinking. But it didn't seem to matter then. In any case I wasn't drinking much in those days – just a few beers.

Anyhow the boss got to know about my late nights. There was always some nosy sod who'd ring him up and say, 'I saw that Georgie Best last night. I thought he was supposed to be a bleeding athlete!' At the start of the '65 season he called me into his office and gave me a lecture. It was the first time Matt had me on the carpet. I was to get used to the experience. That first time I listened to him. He told me I'd been a bloody idiot. I remember him saying, 'You've done the hard bit, son, you've got to the top. Staying there is easy if you only think about it.' He said I'd got in with a wrong crowd, not a bad crowd like crooks or anything, but the wrong crowd for an athlete. He said he'd noticed I'd been tired on the field and that obviously the life I was leading affected my play.

I took it all in. He was right. But I was still a bit pissed off about being bawled out. I've always felt if I want to do something why the hell shouldn't I do it providing it was legal. If I wanted to get laid, fall down drunk, stay up all night, why the fuck shouldn't I? I didn't like the notion that if I pissed in the street it was news and someone told the boss about it. But the guy who told the boss couldn't get arrested if he walked naked down High Street. That made me mad and as time went on I got more and more resentful about it.

Anyway that bollocking from the boss was the first of many. I got so used to being put on the carpet that Matt used to say I was more in his office than he was.

Later when he sent for me I used to sit and look at the wallpaper behind his head. It was funny wallpaper with animals on and I used to count the animals while he gave me a bollocking. I used to want the bollocking to last a long time so I could finish my counting. One day he got really mad at me and went on at some length and I managed to count them all. There are 272 animals on Matt Busby's wallpaper.

I remember seeing that film *Charlie Bubbles* where Albert Finney sat in a conference and shut out all the sound from his ears so that he could see the mouths moving but he wasn't listening. I used to do that with Matt when I wasn't counting animals on wallpaper. And I used to do it when I went to business conferences where they were talking about 'exploiting my commercial potential' and all that bollocks. I used to fill my head with music and remember great games I'd played and nod occasionally. They'd think I was listening but I hadn't heard a word they'd said.

I remember every game I ever played in, good and bad. I've got my own action replay. I can run it through my mind at will. I remember one game when I was in the 'B' team long before I ever got in the first team and we were playing against Blackburn. I remember it was snowing and no one was watching. We were drawing 0—0 at half time and the conditions were atrocious. At half time John Fitzpatrick, one of my team mates, said, 'I'll bet you can't score a goal straight from the kick off'. So I said, 'You're bloody on'.

So we get out on to the pitch and he gives me the ball and I set off and beat about six players and stick it in the bloody net. 'Is that all right?' I said to Fitzy when I got back to the half-way line. You should have seen his face. That gave me a thrill. It still does when I think about it.

Another goal I remember I scored at Chelsea when I was about nineteen. I used to love it there. Their bloody defenders used to have to pay twice to get back into the ground when I'd finished with them. Anyway this particular day I got the ball on our half-way line, gave it to Dave Sadler who was playing centre-forward at the time, and set off for the one-two.

I ran about twenty bloody yards, full tilt, and took the return. It wasn't a good one, it was hard and fast about waist high. I went to volley it with my right, changed my mind and hit it with my left foot. It went into the net like a bloody rocket. I don't know why I changed feet in mid air. Showing off I suppose.

I loved playing to the crowd. I believed I was an entertainer,

'I used to be like a bullfighter, taunting them, inviting them to charge me'

The young George Best:
'the physique of a tooth-
pick and the pallor of a
child raised on chip
butties . . .'

George Best and the hard
men: 'They never used to
bother me because they
weren't very good at it'

Above : 'El Beatel': Best returns from a triumphant European Cup win, and captures the front pages with this picture

Opposite top : Taking on the Liverpool defence in 1966. Sir Matt said 'he had more ways of beating a player than any other player I have ever seen'

Opposite bottom : George Best preening himself before tasting the delights of Manchester's night-life in the mid-sixties

Managers I have known: Sir Matt Busby, 'One of the greatest managers of all time' and George with his European Footballer of the Year trophy, Wilf McGuinness, Frank O'Farrell and Tommy Docherty; for these men the 'Best problem' took on massive proportions

The trappings of success: birds, booze, boutique and a big, white Jag

that people came to see me play and I always tried to put on a show. At least in those early days I did. I loved doing things that meant something to someone in the crowd. You know, like a bull-fighter dedicates an animal to some bird. I used to score goals and do tricks for people.

I remember once when Noel Cantwell was manager of Coventry City and his team were in danger of relegation. The other team in the shit were Notts Forest and we were playing Notts. If we beat them they went down and Coventry stayed up. I always liked Noel. He played at United when I was there and he was always trying to sort me out but I was too daft to listen.

Anyway that night before the game I thought I'm going to stick one in for Noel. He was at the game, I saw him sitting in the stand when we kicked off. Anyway we were losing 1—0 and it was the start of the second half when I got this ball, cut inside and hit it. I knew from the moment it left my foot it was going in. It couldn't have been nearer the angle of the post and bar. I was running toward the stand before it went in the net I was that sure. I stood under where Noel was sitting and gave him a wave and he was laughing with joy. That was a big thrill because I felt like a great bullfighter and I'd given him something.

Then there were the two goals I scored in Lisbon against Benfica. I've scored better goals but I'll always remember that game as being something special for the way I played and the way the team strung it together. For the only time I played for them United were a great side that night. I remember before I went on the field getting excited, getting the horn. I knew I was going to be special that night. They could have had thirty-seven Benfica players in the fucking park and there's no way they were going to stop me.

After five minutes I realized we were all on form and I remember I looked at Paddy and he started laughing because he knew we were going to look a great team and he's laughing like a lunatic at the thought. All of us played that night like we never wanted it to stop. We could have gone on forever. I've got a film of that game and I still play it through. That night we looked like Real Madrid when Puskas and di Stefano played for them.

Funny though how I remember the bad things as well. I still wake up at night even now reliving some of the bloody awful things that happened to me on the field. Once we played Arsenal and they were giving us some hammer and I thought next time it's shit or bust, so, go through on my own and score. So I get the ball, thread through the defence and I've only the keeper, Bob Wilson, to beat. He comes rushing out, dives at my feet and takes the ball from me. Now I still get the raving needle when I relive that moment. I always reckoned that when I got through with only the keeper to beat you could put a million quid on me scoring and you'd be right a hundred times out of a hundred. I still can't fathom what I did wrong that game and it still worries me.

My worst nightmare is when I played in a semi-final against Leeds. It was at the time towards the end of my career when I was boozing too much, not playing well. Also I had serviced a young lady an hour before the game so I wasn't feeling too energetic. (I will tell you about that incident later.) Anyway again I get through the Leeds defence and I'm about forty yards from goal. As I say at that time and in a situation like I've described I was certain to score. But all of a sudden I started thinking about what I should do, where once I just ran through and stuck it in.

Anyway I was thinking about it and I fell over face down in the bloody mud. Nobody near me and I fall over the sodding ball. I still think about it and it annoys me because I got it wrong.

It nearly put me off women.

Nearly, but not quite.

CHAPTER 5

Busby's assessment of the starting point of Best's downfall may be accurate in the sense that the drinking and the late nights started from the very beginning but it is certainly true that it wasn't until some time later, round about 1969–70 in fact, that the consequences became apparent to the general public. Before the slide downhill George Best had still one or two peaks to scale.

In the season 1966–7 following his triumph in Lisbon he was the lynch pin of United's achievement in winning the League title for the second year in the three years since he joined them. Best played in every game, scored ten goals and made one marvel at his precocious skills.

He was also box office. Manchester United's average home gate in 1966–7 was 52 000, an increase of 15 000 on the previous year. It was to stay around that mark so long as George Best was playing.

By winning the League they once more qualified for the European Cup, once more embarked on Busby's dream. This was to be Busby's greatest moment and Best's most spectacular season. He scored twenty-eight goals in the League and played a considerable part in United winning the European Cup.

The path towards it began in farce when United played a Maltese team who lost a player on the way to the first leg. He stopped off to buy an ice cream in London and failed to turn up for the match.

In the quarter finals Gornik Zabrze, the Polish team, provided much sterner opposition, and United had to be at their best to win. After the two legs the Gornik manager, Dr Geza Kaloscai, said, 'If there is a better winger I haven't seen him. Best could have played at any time in any of the world's greatest teams!'

In the semi-finals United played the legendary Real Madrid. In the first leg at Old Trafford Best scored the only goal of the game and everyone reckoned it wasn't enough. It seemed they were right when in the return game in Madrid United were losing 3—1 at half time. Best remembers the dressing room at the interval.

'It was like a bloody morgue. Everybody shattered. I mean we are well stuffed, aren't we? Then in comes the boss. We think we're going to get a right bollocking and we deserved it because we were awful. But he just looks in and says, "Right, lads, go out there and keep playing football". And I started bloody laughing. I mean there's this old bugger who'd give his left arm to win the sodding cup and we're screwing it up for him and he tells us to keep on playing football. I thought that was a bit special.'

Anyway it worked. United went out and attacked and finally achieved the draw and thereby the winning aggregate goal when Best sprinted down the wing and crossed the ball for Foulkes to score.

They were in the final and they played Benfica at Wembley, winning 4—1 after extra time with Best again getting the significant goal in the first minute of extra time. Busby had seen his dream come true and that was the important thing. Best had all his dreams before him, or so it seemed.

He had just completed a season when he had added new dimensions to his already staggering range of gifts. He had merged two life styles, soccer and showbiz, into one. He was an athlete and an entertainer, a soccer player and a sex symbol, an adolescent and a working-class hero.

By middle-class standards he was well off, about £150 a week, two boutiques in Manchester and a fish and chip shop in Belfast which he bought his parents. His fan mail was delivered daily by the sack load and he treated it with marvellous disdain. 'I'd go mad reading it all. I used to. Some of it you wouldn't believe; "Dear George, I want you to fuck me", and that would be one of the nicer ones', he said. He had already published an autobiography called, surprisingly enough, *Best of Both Worlds*, and had appeared on the Eamonn Andrews show.

Other accolades seemingly dropped in his lap. He was voted footballer of the year by polling sixty per cent of the votes and the only question was who on earth did the other forty per cent vote for? In a poll taken by a national newspaper to find the most popular British footballer there were twelve contestants. Best

44

polled six time more votes than the rest put together. The Irish soccer writers, knowing a good thing when they see it, voted him their player of the year as did soccer writers from twenty-four countries in Europe. He became the youngest ever winner of 'le Ballon d'Or' with sixty-one votes. Bobby Charlton was second with fifty-seven votes.

Danny Blanchflower, himself a supreme artist with a football, was asked to place in order of preference Matthews, Finney and Best. Danny voted for George. He reasoned, 'Stanley was a supreme dribbler who would fox even the most ruthless, sophisticated defences. But he was primarily a provider. Finney was perhaps a better all-rounder than Matthews. He could play anywhere in the forward line and besides that was a free goal scorer. But George Best gets my vote. A master of control and manipulation, he is also a superb combination of creator and finisher, he can play anywhere along the line.

'But more than the others he seems to have a wider more appreciative eye for any situation. He seldom passes to a colleague in a poor position. He is prepared to carry the responsibility himself.

'But basically Best makes a greater appeal to the senses than the other two. His movements are quicker, lighter, more balletic. He offers the greater surprise to the mind and the eye. Though you could do nothing about it, you usually knew how Matthews would beat you. In those terms he was more predictable to the audience. Best has the more refined, unexpected range. And with it all is his utter disregard of physical danger.'

He also had a disregard for the accepted patterns of behaviour of an athlete. Even given their new-found prosperity British footballers on the whole were finding it difficult to change their habits. They might be earning a good living but the majority still seemed intent on keeping body and soul together until they had saved enough money for retirement and that little newsagent's business on the corner.

Best was never inhibited by such mundane desires. He made it known he wanted to be a millionaire by the time he was thirty, he was often seen in public places where alcoholic refreshment could be purchased and always nearby some lovely young girl gazing with adoring eyes, as eager as a filly at the starting gate. Wherever he went he was accepted and adored. He became Britain's first playboy soccer player and one imagined him scoring goals with one arm round a film star while flicking through the brochure for a holiday in Majorca. It was not a bad front to present to the world, particularly in a profession lacking in colour, and Best with an instinctive gift for self-publicity gave every indication of wallowing in it.

He went to Majorca for a holiday and flew home for a business deal. He told the press he came home for a haircut. The headlines said: 'A £56 trim for Best'.

Whichever pub or discothèque he patronized immediately became Manchester's most popular nightspot. Whichever girl he dated, no matter how obscure, made the gossip columns. He went on television and said he would never kiss a person who smoked. Two-packs-a-day girls wrote and said they'd never touch another cigarette. So did a few men. Best's appeal was universal.

I was living in Manchester in those days and saw a lot of George Best. I marvelled at his seeming ability to cope with the most formidable distractions, his patience with people who interrupted his private moments simply to be rude or boorish. He knew better than most that he had embarked on a long walk on a tight-rope. To keep the correct balance between the demands of the athlete and the trappings of showbiz was going to take some doing.

Moreover he knew he had to do it himself. There was no precedent, no one in the game who could understand him and his problems and thereby guide him.

He had an agent, but he lived in Huddersfield and was hardly likely to have an intimate knowledge of the discothèque scene in London and Manchester. His parents were in Belfast and in any event who could expect them to understand what was happening to their son? It was beyond their comprehension. Similarly it was bigger than Matt Busby for in all his mountain of experience in soccer he had never handled a player so lionized and seduced by influences outside of the game.

In the beginning George Best seemed in control of the situation. But gradually he changed. By the age of twenty-one the madcap exuberance, the almost childlike joy of having so many good things, had been replaced by a more wary, much more circumspect attitude. He had the ability to be forever at the centre of things and yet remain private and remote. His appraisal of people around him remained cool and in the main shrewd.

Contrary to popular opinion Best's friends, by whom I mean the people really close to him not just the fringe associates, have been remarkable for their loyalty and devotion. In his very darkest moments when he seemed hell-bent on self-destruction it was these friends who pulled him back from the edge and tried to protect him from recurring black moods.

By the time he was twenty-three Best was pretty bored with his life style. He could see the frustrating contradictions more clearly than most. The social scene in Manchester which clung to his coat tail sounded glamorous at a distance. In fact it was tiny and parochial. He was a jet-setter with an agent in Huddersfield, a superstar earning £30000 a year and living in digs in Chorlton-cum-Hardy. He was a glamour puss who was supposed to live like a monk, a swinger expected to do everything in moderation. He had a Rolls-Royce and he parked it outside a semi-detached in a suburb of Manchester. He soon discovered that Manchester was a tiny village in which his every movement was observed and remarked.

Most days Sir Matt would get a phone call from a supposed supporter alleging that Best had been seen in this or that drinking club and what was the manager going to do about it?

'I used to tell them when they complained, what do you expect me to do, sleep with the player?'

George Best would most certainly not have approved of that notion.

Matt had one other idea to give his troubled star a new purpose in life – why didn't Georgie settle down and get married?

*   *   *

GEORGE'S STORY

The boss was always going on at me about getting married and settling down. So one day I thought I'd try it and see what it was like. Since I made it big in soccer I never had any difficulty with women. They used to fall over themselves to get into bed with me. I'm not daft and I don't kid myself. I know that a lot of them just did it to say they had slept with George Best. They are what are known as starfuckers. I could always tell them because just as they were going to climb into bed with me they'd say, 'I hope you don't think I'm doing this just because you are George Best'.

I didn't mind so long as I enjoyed myself. Once I met a bird who was really hot for me but I left her alone because I had a feeling she was too young. Two days later I got a call from her mother. She said, 'You know my daughter is only fifteen, don't you'? I said I thought as much and thanked her. 'Never mind, she'll be sixteen in two months', she said.

I once had a girl who tried to sleep with me so she could write about it for a newspaper. One day I got a phone call from a mate, a journalist, who said I'd be contacted by a bird who would say she was a journalist and wanted an interview. In fact this bird was on the game and had been paid £1500 by a newspaper to go to bed with me so she could write about it. Sure enough this bird rang me a day or so later. I told her to get stuffed. But the more I thought about it the more I got the needle – £1500 to sleep with me.

Christ, I'm not that bad.

I knew some birds who didn't need paying – all of them in fact, except for this girl I was supposed to marry. It happened in 1969. We were touring Denmark just prior to our season starting. I was in the hotel waiting for the coach to take us to the airport when this big blonde bird came up and asked for my autograph. You could say I fell in love with a pair of knockers. Anyway I thought she was sensational.

She slipped away before I could talk to her so I wrote a letter addressed to 'My Danish Dream Girl' and gave it to a Danish newspaperman. He put the story in the papers, asking the girl to contact me. I got four replies from birds all claiming to be the one, but when I asked for photographs I got the real one. Her name was Eva Haraldsted. I asked her to come to England. I thought she might make a good model. I also thought she was a very tasty bird.

I met her at London airport and took her to a hotel. Separate rooms because I wasn't sure of the lie of the land. Anyway I soon try it out but she isn't having any. It ends up with me stark bollock naked chasing her down the corridor of the hotel. She's only got a pair of pants and a bra on.

I always remember we passed this old geezer in the corridor cleaning shoes and he just looks up and says, 'Good evening, sir', as we run by. It was like a scene from one of those Brian Rix plays. Anyway, nothing, sweet f.a. So next day I take her to Manchester and gradually things turn out all right.

I told her I loved her, but then I told most of them that at one time or another. But she took it seriously and started talking about engagements and marriage. One or two newspapers got on to the story and I must admit I told them Eva and I had talked about marriage. We never got engaged but we'd talked about a house and settling down and all that.

I soon got fed up though. I didn't really know what to do because of the publicity and all that. Anyway one day a certain lady journalist came up for an interview. What I used to do with lady journalists was ask them to call at one of the boutiques so that the lads could take a good look at her. If she was fair looking they'd ring me and tell me. If she was a drag I wouldn't bother.

Anyway they rang me and said she was a looker so I went into the boutique and right enough she was fair. So she set off asking me the usual twenty questions that every journalist had ever asked me and I was wondering how I could pull her. She asked me about Eva and getting married and I said, 'Oh, we'll have to see about that. I might change my mind.' All of a sudden she's got a story. She goes off and rings her office and says, 'The office says I've got to stick with you. Can't let you out of my sight.' So I said, 'It'll get a bit cramped in Mrs Fullaway's single bed'.

In the end we didn't use Mrs Fullaway's single bed.

I liked that journalist. Every time she wanted a story she used to come and stay with me in Manchester.

That's what I call good press relations.

Anyway Eva's not pleased with the story, is she? She goes bloody spare! Eventually she sues me for breach of promise. I settled out of court. It cost me £500. I've never paid for it since.

Poor old Matt. He always wanted me to get married but he reckoned I went about it the wrong way. When it was announced that I was going to get married to her he went berserk. He had me in his office and said, 'What's all this about you marrying a girl you've only known a matter of weeks. And a foreign girl too. Why can't you be like everyone else and marry someone nearer home?' I tried to tell him that I wasn't like everyone else. That circumstances made me different.

I didn't tell him because I didn't know how to say it without seeming big-headed.

But even if I had I wonder if he'd have understood.

CHAPTER 6

A prime reason for me wanting to be successful in business without
having to work myself by the time I reach twenty-four, is that I will
then be able to concentrate solely on becoming the world's best footballer. At twenty-four I expect to have arrived at a nice financial
situation. I should like to have a man to clean my shoes, another to drive
me about and other people to look after my personal and financial
affairs.

GEORGE BEST: *Best of Both Worlds*, published 1968

Huddersfield is in Yorkshire, between Leeds and Manchester.
It is a town dedicated to common sense and thrift and looks it.
There is something four-square, solid, virtuous, even smug about
Huddersfield. St George's Square is at its centre and Ken Stanley's
office overlooks the square. Stanley is a guardedly friendly man,
small and in the fifties, given nowadays to smoking heavily and the
odd nervous twitch.

1974 was not exactly a good year for Ken Stanley. As agent for
the English football team he was less than enchanted when it failed
to qualify for the Munich World Cup. For, in addition to being a
sports agent, Stanley is also heavily involved in merchandising
sports goods – everything from soccer coaching strips for newspapers to shoulder bags with 'England – World Cup Munich 74'
written on them. He has a warehouse full of bags like that.

On top of that George Best had announced for the third and
presumably final time that he had finished with football. George
Best was Ken Stanley's most famous client. 'Let's be fair – he was
seventy-five per cent of my business', he says with beguiling
honesty. 1974 is a year which Stanley would willingly erase from
the calendar.

The sports agent is a newcomer to the field of merchandising

51

athletes. With increasing interest in sporting events by the media – particularly television – and the consequent interest from commercial companies in the exploitation of athletes, the agents have become important figures. Golf, tennis and motor racing are three sports where the participants' rewards have considerably increased as a result of certain agents realizing the commercial opportunities and exploiting them to the utmost.

By comparison soccer, in Britain at least, has lagged behind other sports in the realization of its full commercial potential. The Football Association and the Football League, the twin executives of the sport, are notoriously conservative by nature and some of their members are still too busy debating the abolition of the maximum wage and the length of players' hair to turn their minds to the necessity, or otherwise, of agents.

It has led to some curious anomalies. For instance agents are not allowed to negotiate a contract on behalf of their clients with the clubs that employ them and there is little doubt that because of this some clubs get away with paying their stars a lot less than they are worth.

Best is the classic example.

The most he ever earned from United as a player was just over £11 000 a year and this was not until his last year or so with the club when Frank O'Farrell was the manager. Of course he earned more but the rest was comprised of bonuses that had to be worked for and might or might not be achieved.

The consequence of this is that in world terms British soccer players are, on the whole, poorly paid. The stars, like Best, were paid peanuts. In fact when Best was arguably the world's greatest player and certainly its most valuable commercial property he was probably not among the top twenty best-paid players in the game. Top Italian players, for instance, earn in excess of £30 000 and Eusebio, the Portuguese player, earned £20 000 a year from the club. That in a country where the average wage is around £600 a year shows the difference between Best's earnings and the rest of football's super stars.

If one takes into account Best's drawing power at his peak, the number of people who went to see him – and only him – both home and away, then he should have been earning £40 000 to £50 000 a year, from the game alone. If that sounds excessive one should take into account that the receipts at Wembley for the 1974 Cup Final watched by 100 000 people was a staggering £240 000.

Given the present situation where agents must sit on the touchlines while their clients negotiate their own basic contracts, they concentrate their energies on activities outside of soccer. Ken Stanley didn't have much difficulty selling George Best. Everyone wanted George Best. Ken Stanley's job was finding him.

He was introduced to Best nearly ten years ago, shortly after the player had made the first team. Denis Law, Stanley's first client, brought him along. Stanley, at the time, was more an agent manqué than an agent proper.

He had started his career as a table tennis player, good one too, touring the country with players like Richard Bergman. He ran a five-a-side football hall in Lancashire before moving to Huddersfield to work with a company manufacturing sports goods. He signed Law and started dealing on the telephone from home.

Then George Best happened.

'I remember the kid standing there. So shy and reserved and I wondered about him. But then he blossomed and he was the biggest thing we've ever seen', he says.

Within a year or so of their meeting, George Best Esq. became George Best Associates and George Best Enterprises. Stanley operated from a spacious suite of offices. Three girls were employed to handle George's mail. At its peak it reached 10 000 letters a week. The George Best fan club was started. It soon had a membership of 15 000 with flourishing branches in Moscow and Tokyo.

'The mail was incredible. Some of the letters from the females you wouldn't believe. And then there were the worrying ones. The ones begging for money and asking for George to heal them of some illness by touching them. It was frightening', said Stanley.

It was also big business. Twenty thousand copies of the George Best annual, indistinguishable from any others except for his name, were printed and sold out within three days, at £1 a copy. Future issues sold 120 000 copies. He was offered a part in the film version of *The Virgin Soldiers*. He had to turn it down. The BBC made a fifty-minute documentary called 'The World of George Best'. He starred in a series of coaching films which ran for twenty weeks on BBC TV and was sold all over the world. He advertised cosmetics, football books, plastic footballs, men's clothes, eggs for the Egg Marketing Board. His face was on everything from pop posters, to tea mugs, to packets of chewing gum.

He was also big news. Whatever he did, whatever he said, was reported along with a lot of what he neither did nor said. His appeal was universal, cutting through social and intellectual barriers. The mobs at the back of the goals loved him and identified with him, pubescent girls and some who ought to have known better scratched messages of love on his car and stood outside his shops and swooned when he passed by.

The intellectuals and the trendies, those pot-bellied, prematurely middle-aged creatures who previously had looked down their noses at soccer as a mere diversion for the hoi-polloi, invited him to their dinner parties. Women who were not renowned for throwing themselves at men made him a target.

On the whole he took it all with exceptional cool. One woman, married, beautiful and quite intelligent, told me a marvellous story about Best which summed him up at this point in his career. She met him at a party and was immediately attracted to him.

'He had the most marvellous eyes and a shy boyish charm. I talked to him for a long time and entertained thoughts of seducing him. I wondered how I might go about it. We talked for about half an hour and all the time I fantasized an affair with him. All of a sudden a blonde girl came up to him. She said, "Hi, I'm Julie, would you like a quick fuck?" He said, "Certainly". He turned to me and said, "Excuse me", and went upstairs with her.'

He was God's gift to journalism and, again, it didn't matter what kind of periodical it was, it wanted something on George.

The Sunday Times Magazine, a journal whose interest in soccer could justly be described as peripheral, devoted two pages to full-length pictures of Best wearing only a pair of shorts to illustrate an article describing the injuries sustained by a top-class soccer player. When the photographs had been taken and before they were published I was telephoned by *The Sunday Times* to give advice on the pictures.

'There are some marks on his neck that he says were caused by a defender's elbows. Is that likely?' I was asked. 'I should leave it out,' I said. I saw him later and said, 'Which defender was it who put those marks on your neck?' 'Can't remember, but she doesn't play for a first division club', he said.

While *The Sunday Times* saw Best as a battered glamour boy, the *Morning Star* portrayed him, quite correctly, as the new working-class hero. The writer Stanley Levenson said, 'The footballer is no longer the hired hand who knows his place. He is more independent, more public, more exposed to newspapers and television.'

He sold his two boutiques and the rights to the use of his name on men's and boys' clothing for £25 000. Harold Tillman, who made the deal, planned to open George Best boutiques on the continent. An impresario wanted him to tour the clubs doing a ball-juggling act for £1000 a week. Newspaper and magazine colour and instructional strips bearing his name were syndicated throughout the world. Without really trying he was earning between £40 000 and £50 000 a year. His ambition to be a millionaire by the age of thirty was well within his grasp. Ken Stanley hired an accountant to deal exclusively with Best's financial affairs.

All Best had to do was reap the golden harvest. Instead he put a torch to it. The incident with Eva Haraldsted suing for breach of promise and a subsequent brawl in a nightclub ending in a court case hardly endeared him to advertisers aiming at a clean-cut image for the kiddy winkies.

From 1970 onwards Best's behaviour both on and off the field deteriorated to such an extent that it would be hard to find a product befitting his image beyond cut-throat razors or do-it-yourself suicide kits.

But even before 1970 Best had shown a curiously casual approach to the advertising men considering his avowed intent to be a thirty-year-old millionaire. He simply never turned up for some of the biggest deals. He was offered £50 000 to do one advertisement. He turned it down. 'Why?' I asked. 'Couldn't be bothered having

55

lunch, spending time with people I didn't fancy,' he said. He reckons he turned down at least £250000 of advertising because he 'couldn't be bothered'.

Ken Stanley remains curiously cagey about his client's earnings. He retains a fond notion that Best might yet repent, change his ways and come back to soccer. 'Image is very important to George, you know', he said. That same week Best admitted in a newspaper to having an illegitimate child.

'I still like the boy, you know, in spite of the problems and the difficulties. I've never seen him lose his temper, he's always been charming and obliging. In fact' – and here Ken Stanley chose his words carefully – 'he could charm the arse off an elephant.'

Best's financial prospects were, in fact, quite remarkable and all he had to do was be sensible until he was thirty. Ken Stanley shakes his head in wonderment at the simplicity of the equation and the fact that his client seemed unable to grasp it. 'Once after he had run away and left everyone in the lurch and had come back I had a talk to him and said, "George, don't you like me?" "Of course I like you," he said. "You wouldn't bloody think so the way you go on," I said.

'Another time when Matt called me in after George had run away again I remember Matt saying to George, "Look, that's Ken Stanley and he's your agent. Any problems outside soccer go to him. That's what you pay him for. I'm your manager. Any problems, personal or professional, come to me. We'll look after you and all you have to do is keep fit, live like an athlete and you can retire when you are thirty if you want. Now does that seem too difficult?"

' "Yes," said George.'

Stanley makes the valid point that Best never came to terms with his fame in the sense that he was unable to translate it into power.

'I mean at the time he was potentially one of the most powerful men in Britain. He could go anywhere, do anything. He could walk up to the Lord Mayor of Manchester and say, "Close the city down for ten minutes while I have a think", and he'd bloody well have done it.

'On a more practical level he could have used the access he had to people to his own advantage. I mean Harold Wilson used to write him bloody fan letters. George didn't even answer them. On the other hand David Frost had Harold Wilson to breakfast and the like. Clever lad, that David Frost. That's what George should have done.'

Stanley's disappointment with his client is in no way alleviated by what he sees as a new and expanding market for soccer. 'Soccer as a world game is only just starting. Think what will happen when the bloody Chinese start playing it and all the African nations. Think of the commercial possibilities then. That's what I used to say to George but half the time he wouldn't listen.'

Best himself says that he is not really certain now why he so casually rejected such easy pickings. 'I think I couldn't be bothered. I really only lived for soccer and I thought the rest was a load of crap. I remember once they sent a helicopter for me to take me to London for a day's filming. I was to get £40000 for the advert or something daft.

'They put me in this hotel and told me to be on location next morning at eight. No chance. I just went off and spent the night with a bird. Eventually they found me and I did the advert in the end. I think it used to bore me to think about it, and then when it came to it I couldn't face it.'

Hugh McIlvanney of *The Observer*, one of Britain's most perceptive journalists and a writer with a real insight into Best, has a more interesting and likely theory. In April 1970 he wrote:

'I suspect that deep in his nature there is a strong self-destructive impulse. The Celts, whether Irish, or Welsh, or Scots, whether sportsmen or artists or politicians, have always been pretty strong in the self-destructive department. If hell did not exist the Celts would have invented it. Sometimes I think they did.

'With George Best I have frequently had the impression that he felt uncomfortable when things were going too well. He likes to imagine himself an unashamed sybarite and must therefore reject such an interpretation of his psychology but his protests do not convince me.

'No one whose profoundest craving is for the sweet and easy life would provoke the fates as consistently as he does. Now and again, at completely arbitrary moments, he appears to have an irresistible desire to put two fingers up to the whole world.'

The accuracy of McIlvanney's prediction can be seen in hindsight because from the very moment he wrote the article Best was embarked on a seemingly self-destructive scheme to wreck his career.

Ken Stanley offers no such profundities. He takes a ruler between his hands and says, 'Look at it this way. This ruler is a footballer's lifespan. The middle three inches is the only time he works and earns. Simple, isn't it? But George couldn't see it. Not him. He could have conquered the world. Do you know that? And then there's China and Africa. Oh dear, what a wasted opportunity.

'I used to say to him, "Why can't you be like Tom Finney? Now there was a player. There was someone who knew how to look after himself. I mean if you're an athlete, you have to respect your body, don't you?"'

Ken Stanley sits in a suite of offices with two girls to help. His attractive daughter sits next door, facing a framed coloured photograph of George Best. In a store room, once filled with George Best products, there is one George Best lampshade and a pile of programmes for an indoor tournament bearing his name and which never happened. The offices overlooking St George's Square, Huddersfield, are quiet and full of ghosts.

Ken Stanley says, 'Perhaps if I had lived nearer him things might have been different. I don't know though. He's a funny fellow.'

He had nearly ten years with George Best and he seemed as if he didn't know whether to laugh or cry about it.

*   *   *

GEORGE'S STORY

The drinking wasn't a problem at first. When you're nineteen or twenty you can get pissed on a few drinks and it doesn't seem to matter. That's how it started with me. I had one golden rule, I never went out on Friday night. Even at the end when I'd finished

I used to stop in on Fridays. Funny how habits stick. I used to drink vodka and lemonade because it looked like nothing and if any nosy sod rang the boss up and told him he'd seen me drinking in a club I could always say it was lemonade.

I always found it difficult to stay at home nights with a good book or whatever. Perhaps that is what I should have done but it used to bore the arse off me. It still does. I like moving around, I like action.

When I was seventeen or eighteen I used to love being recognized. It was a marvellous feeling to walk down a street knowing everyone was looking at you and wishing they were in your shoes. Later on I would have given anything to go somewhere and be anonymous.

It got to be a real problem. I could only go to the odd pub or club where I knew I'd be protected by the owner and even then I'd have to take someone with me. Because if I stood at a bar by myself having a quiet drink you can bet some boring fart would come along and want to talk about soccer.

If I went to the movies I used to have to go in after the film had started and leave before the lights went up at the end. I never saw the end of a film for about seven years. The birds I took out casually loved all the recognition but the regular girl friends soon got pissed off.

I remember one regular pulling a right moody when I took her to this Italian restaurant where the guy took my coat and helped me into my chair and completely ignored her. But no matter where you went you'd always get aggravation. There would always be someone who would want to take you on. At first I used to walk away from it and try to ignore it. Later I used to argue and get into trouble. I'll give you an example.

One day I'm standing at the bar with a few of the lads having a drink and this fella about six feet four high and three feet across comes across to me and bangs his pint pot on the counter and says he's gonna smash my head to pulp. I've never seen him before so I ask him why he is going to whack me and he comes out with some incredible story about his mate's brother had told him I had ogled his wife in a pub two weeks ago.

What do you say to a fella like that?

Fortunately the guy who owns the pub comes across and says to the big guy, 'Any more aggro and I'll whack you with this', and he opens his jacket and there's a bloody big truncheon dangling down his side. So the fella calms down. Then, a few minutes later, he comes across and says he wants to apologize. Like I say once when I was younger I would have accepted, but by now I am sick of all the aggro so I tell him to piss off. So it starts all over again and they have to smuggle me out of the back door.

One day I was driving through Manchester, and I had stopped at the traffic lights. I'm parked there minding my own business when this guy walks by and says, 'You are a big-headed twat'. Again I thought, leave it, he's an idiot. Then I thought why should I back down to him? So I pretended I'd not heard. I wound the window down and said, 'Sorry, mate, I didn't hear you'. So he walked up to the window and was about to repeat his statement when I leaned back and whacked him straight on the nose. Then I drove off. I left him in the middle of two lanes of traffic with his nose all over his face.

Later, a mate of mine in Manchester, a bit of a villain, rang me up and said the geezer I'd hit had been trying to get one or two fellas to duff me up. My mate had gone to him and said that if I so much as caught a cold he would be held responsible and chopped into little pieces. I knew some nice characters in Manchester.

Actually the women were the worst with the aggro. They either wanted to go to bed with me or they wanted to insult me. I remember once going to see Tommy Cooper at a club. I crept in after the show had started but at the interval they put the house lights up and I was spotted. There was a huge crowd of old ladies at the show. It must have been a works outing or a Darby and Joan Club trip or something.

Anyway they all came over and asked for autographs and I signed every one. Then bugger me I've just settled back to enjoy the show when an old dear comes back with the paper I've autographed, flings it on the table in front of me, screaming, 'How do you expect my grandson to read that?' and whacks me across the head with a handbag. Now what do you make of that?

In the end these kinds of pressures used to get me down. Whereas once I'd get silly drunk, I'd just get nasty drunk because I knew that someone would try something bloody silly. I've always been a bit of a mad Irish sod and before things went sour I pulled some right strokes. For instance when I won the Footballer of the Year Award I was so chuffed with the trophy I wouldn't let go of it.

Naturally enough I had a few vodkas with some of the lads and I remember we went to a nightclub and I got up on stage and danced with the chorus girls and I was still clutching my player of the year award.

Then me and a mate picked up two darling birds and they took us back to their flat and I went into the bedroom with my bird and she started getting undressed. I remember her standing in front of a mirror brushing her hair. It was long and black and she had a marvellous figure. I was that drunk I was standing there wondering how to get undressed without letting go of my award.

Eventually I decided I could manage it sitting down so I went to sit on the bed, missed it by four feet and ended up lying on the floor. I remember the bird looking down at me, starkers, and saying, 'Some player of the year'. Then I fell asleep.

I woke up still clutching my award and staggered out of the flat. I hadn't a bloody clue where I was. It was dawn and it was raining so I stood in a doorway waiting for a taxi. After a while I sat down and fell asleep. I woke up with someone shaking me. It was a policeman.

He said, 'What are you doing here?' and I said like a dozy sod, 'I'm the player of the year'.

'Bloody looks like it,' he said. 'What's that?' he said and he pointed to the parcel under my arm.

I told him it was my trophy.

'Show us then,' he said. And I did.

'Very nice too,' he said, 'but I'd go back to your hotel if I were you otherwise you'll get pneumonia and the award will be posthumous.'

He got me a cab and sent me home.

'Well done,' he said as I got in the cab.

There were times when it helped to be famous.

There were times ahead when the police wanted me on official business.

CHAPTER 7

One thing his detractors can never accuse George Best of is not heeding their advice. They urged him to get married and he got halfway there, they warned him about 'burning the candle at both ends' and, from time to time, he extinguished at least one flame. He was told to forget his business interests and concentrate on his football which he did so frequently that his agent had to spend most of his time looking for his client.

Best knew better than most that such advice was mere sophistry when applied to his own case. But at least he went through the motions.

Another specious piece of advice he received was to find a nice homely girl – nothing flash – buy a house and settle down. He rejected the first half as being totally out of character, but the part about buying a home of his own filled him with strange enthusiasm. He nearly convinced himself that a house was the answer to most of his problems. In fact, it became a monument to them. No single episode in his life so illustrates the predicament he was in.

To begin with it wasn't just a simple matter of building a house and then walking through the front door. He had first to get the permission of the club. Like most footballers, and certainly all Manchester United players, he was bound by contract to live in digs until he was married! It didn't matter that Best was earning £50000 a year, that he was an international star, that he was inevitably forever on display and therefore in need of a retreat.

They were adamant that Best should live with Mrs Fullaway on a council estate in Chorlton and park his Rolls-Royce in the street outside.

For a long time, of course, Best had ignored the rule. To all intents and purposes he lodged at Mrs Fullaway's. In fact he slept in more beds than a travelling salesman and several restaurants in

Manchester would have been in difficulties had he stopped eating out. But he was tiring of the nomadic life and wanted a proper home.

Typically he set about providing one without asking the club's permission. Originally he felt he needed a house in the country, an old cottage in fact. Then he settled for a house of ultra-modern design to be built on a site at Bramhall, a 'desirable' suburb of Manchester with the virtue of being near to the club and the airport.

It was the kind of site a young company executive would choose to give himself easy access to town and to provide his family with a glimpse of the countryside. It was these same virtues – easy access from town and a glimpse of the distant Pennines – that were to make the site one of Britain's most popular tourist attractions – once the house was built and the new owner was in residence.

But even before that happened George Best's house was news. From the very first announcement that he was thinking of having a house built to the moment he moved in, what was designed as his private retreat had become public property.

A local architect, Frazer Crane, was given the job of designing Britain's most sophisticated bachelor pad. Crane's finished building was constructed on two levels with the main living areas of the house on the first floor. The ground floor had a spacious garage entrance, a billiards room and a bedroom and bathroom for the resident housekeeper. Upstairs was the main living room described by Best at the time, 'The second most important room in the house. I wanted a spacious interior where I could relax, entertain and listen to music.' The room was L-shaped and enclosed on two sides by floor to ceiling glass panels.

It gave a lovely view of the Pennines, it also gave the day trippers a lovely view of George Best.

The bedroom, where he now did most of his best work, incorporated a bathroom with a plunge bath large enough and deep enough to warrant an attendant, done in red and white mosaic – Manchester United's colours. Outside, the house had a mature orchard and a goldfish pond.

Just before he moved in Best was quoted as saying, 'When I get

home I want somewhere restful and soothing. I suppose it is because my life is frantic and noisy and I want a home which is a
complete contrast.' In fact he would have been more private living
in a floodlit phone booth, as he soon found out.

He moved in around about the autumn of 1970 without demur
from the club which by now had settled into a policy of letting
George do just about anything he wanted so long as he turned out
for them on Saturday. The event did not, however, go unremarked
by the press.

The Times gave half a page to a description of the house
based on the premise contained in the opening sentence of the
article, 'What happens when a twenty-three-year-old footballer
decides to commission a firm of architects to design his first
house?'

The snobbism inherent in that remark was mild compared with
another report in the *Daily Mirror*. I reprint it in all its pristine
glory.

Sunday trippers in their hundreds turned up yesterday to see the house
that George Best built. The visitors peeped through the windows,
gazed into the fishpond, tramped around the garden and climbed the
outside verandah stairs to get a closer look.

And in the end most of them reached the same embarrassing conclusion about the white tiled residence in Blossom Lane, Bramhall, Cheshire.

It reminded them of a loo.

The Manchester United soccer idol was away for the day from his
new house designed to his own specification and reputed to be costing
him more than £35000.

One of the visitors, Miss Ethel Deakin, 39, of Manchester Road,
Burnage, Lancs, said, 'It's lovely inside, but outside it's just too much.
I was told I couldn't miss it because it looked like a public convenience
and I agree.'

A dog brought along by one of the visitors obviously agreed too. It
eyed George's gleaming tiles, deliberately raised its leg and took a
liberty.

The *News of the World* ran a competition for their readers to
name the house. They received a thousand fit to print and from
these George discounted any to do with soccer such as 'Off-side',

'Left-wing', 'Soccer Haven', 'Goal Holme' and the like and chose 'Che Sera'. Miss E. Bardsley, of Manchester, received £10 for her inspiration.

The *Daily Express* persuaded Best to let them pay for the house-warming party in return for exclusive rights. Richard Burton and Elizabeth Taylor said they couldn't make it to Bramhall, as did Tony Curtis and Pierre Trudeau. Harold Wilson declined on behalf of Mary and himself but added: 'Delighted to see you're in such splendid form again, but to hit the crossbar from thirty-five yards in the last five minutes is a bit much.'

Tommy Trinder did arrive. 'I remember this place when it was the Odeon,' he told the reporters waiting outside the building. Imogen Hassall, who never misses a première, was another guest, as were several other nubile young ladies – including Misses United Kingdom and Great Britain – whose sole contribution to the evening was to push their breasts and bare their teeth at the *Daily Express* photographers who worked throughout with the detachment of anthropologists observing the mating habits of a group of tipsy chimpanzees.

George Best went to bed early, not, it must be said, in protest at the guest list but rather in support of it.

Dick Best, his dad, caused a minor furore by announcing a preference for Guinness when offered champagne. Three security men controlled the doors and outside policemen patrolled to control crowds and traffic. Later these same policemen were the subject of an official investigation following a complaint that a panda car was used to carry drinks from a public house to the house-warming party.

The investigation came to naught except that George Best's house-warming became a matter for public controversy rather than private enjoyment.

The most that can be said for his first few weeks in residence is that at least it provided a change. The worst was that the publicity the house had been given – publicity which always included the address – soon gave it the appeal of a stately home.

Busloads of sightseers started arriving from all over England. The slightly better-off would bring the family car, park it nearby, and sit all afternoon gazing at the smoked glass windows of George Best's lounge.

Best recalls: 'It was unbelievable. After a few weeks I wished I was back in digs. At least a council house in Chorlton was harder to find than my place. I'll never understand why people came and just sat there hour after hour gawping at a house. I don't know if they expected me to stand up and give them a quick flash or something.

'There were always some people around no matter what day you think of but Sundays were the worst. I thought at one time of opening a little stall selling cups of tea, sandwiches, hot dogs and the like. Or charging a parking fee. If I went out on a Sunday I could never get back in. I used to have to ask them to move their bloody cars from the approach to my house.'

The longer he stayed, the more intolerable living at 'Che Sera' became. His fishpond with its fifty goldfish had to be replenished after every weekend. Best wondered who was taking them and the mystery wasn't solved until a local teacher rang him to say that a gang of lads were selling George Best's goldfish every Monday at the school.

The teacher was not offering restitution, he was simply querying the validity of his pupils' claim.

A man came and left an armchair on George Best's front lawn. Best was tempted to release a news story saying that he had found £500 in pound notes concealed in the chair. 'With any amount of luck that would have given the bastard a heart attack', he said.

The women were the worst. 'I used to get all sorts of women at the door. I'd get women who came during the day saying their daughters had pictures of me all over their bedroom walls and could she bring the daughter to the house so I could tell her not to be so daft. Then I'd get the young girls arriving at the door. If I liked them I'd have them in. If I didn't I'd tell them to shove off. I had two sixteen-year-olds used to arrive regularly. Used to tell their parents they were going to the youth club, then come to my place. You wouldn't believe what they got up to.

'Then I had a bird used to drive up from Leicester every week.

Married she was and wanted me to sleep with her. Never did because she was really ugly. They used to make all kinds of excuses to get in the front door. They'd ring the doorbell and when I answered it they'd say, "Oh, is Mavis in?" And then they'd say, "Oh, aren't you George Best?" All that shit used to go on.

'The best was a blonde girl who arrived once and said, "My car's just broken down outside your house. Can I use your phone to call the AA?" I let her in because she was a fair looker. Then I had her on the carpet in the hallway before the AA man arrived. Gave her a quick repair job.

'In the end it got on my fucking nerves. I'd open my bedroom curtains in the morning and there would be a line of young birds looking through the window. It got so I wouldn't answer the phone. I had an ansaphone installed. When the doorbell rang I used to stay quiet and pretend I wasn't in and I used to hide behind curtains so the rubberneckers couldn't see me through the windows.

It was mad. I became a prisoner in my own bloody house. I wanted to turn the whole bloody thing round so I faced away from the road and so they couldn't see me. Sort of turn my back on them.'

Instead of having the rehabilitative effect on Best that his advisers intended, the house undoubtedly emphasized his predicament and increased his frustration and anguish. He went back to his nomadic life, living in friends' flats, coming back to 'Che Sera' only when he had nowhere else to go.

From the moment he went to live there he began his rapid descent downhill.

He sold the house for £40000 when he retired from football.

It was advertised as 'ex-soccer player George Best's luxurious house'.

Today he lives in digs with Mrs Fullaway and parks his Ferrari in the road outside.

*　　*　　*

GEORGE'S STORY

If I'd have been born ugly you would never have heard of Pele. I don't mean that women weakened me or anything like that, I simply mean that without them I might have concentrated more on the game and therefore lasted longer in the game.

The other thing about women weakening you is nonsense. Sometimes when I've played after having a woman I've played marvellously, other times like a big Jessie – so you really can't make rules about it.

Some people have said that I'd have been a better player and might have been more satisfied with life and less unsettled had I been playing my international career with a more successful team than Northern Ireland. There might be something in that but on the other hand I doubt if I would have had as much fun.

The Irish team, on the whole, was a joke. The selectors used to pick a new player then they'd come to me in the dressing room and say, 'Which is the new lad?' But for all that we used to have some right laughs and I used to enjoy meeting up with the Ferret.

Now he was so called because of certain curious habits he possessed such as turning up in the unlikeliest places, roaming up and down corridors at night trying door handles, always sniffing around very quietly. The Ferret was always the first to suggest a good scene.

What he used to do when we went away on international tours was try to organize a situation whereby I got a bird in bed and the rest watched from wardrobes or behind curtains or whatever.

Needless to say the management knew nothing about this. Sometimes they worked, sometimes they didn't but the Ferret was always to the fore.

We set one up in Cyprus once. I had this air hostess and one of the stewards had an adjoining room so we persuaded him to let us have it so we could set up a little scene. We planned to leave the door ajar and then have people standing on chairs and some lying on the floor looking in. We spent a lot of time setting it up.

I had to get the lighting right in the room where I was so all the lads could see and we tested the door to see how far it could open before the bird rumbled. It was all set and then we had to call it off because Billy Bingham, the team manager, must have sensed something was up and patrolled up and down the corridor outside the room.

We'd charged 50p each for that and we had to refund the money.

There was nothing dirty in it. It was just a big laugh for the lads. The girls never knew and I'd have screwed them in any case, so what's the difference?

The funniest scene we had was in Scotland. I got the girl and I had a room with a big bay window. So we got four or five of the lads organized. There were two tall ones and they had to stand up so they were curved like bananas. The Ferret was on his hands and knees along with another couple of lads, all peering through a crack in the curtain.

Anyway I got this girl back in the room and put the wireless on. I did that so she wouldn't hear the lads if they coughed or creaked or anything because if I was on form it could last an hour and the lads had to stay quiet.

So I get going with this bird and she doesn't want to know. Nothing. I've been at it forty-five minutes and I'm nowhere. It should have been a right laugh and it's a flop. Then I thought it's not that much of a flop because the lads have been there quiet and nice for all that time and they must be very stiff so I'll do something really evil. So I switched the wireless off and told the bird I was going downstairs to get her a taxi.

So I left her in the bedroom with these footballers stuck behind the bloody curtains. Apparently after about five minutes this bird gets up and walks across to the dressing table right next to this window and starts brushing her hair.

One of the lads couldn't hold it any longer and he started to giggle. She heard him, gets hold of her umbrella and starts sticking it in the curtain. Then she pulls the curtain back and there's two fellows bent like bananas and two on their hands and knees including the Ferret.

She says, 'You dirty bastards. What are you doing there?'

And the Ferret says, 'We are cleaning the windows. What do you think we are doing?'

At that point I came in the room just as the lads are piling out.

I said, as innocently as I could, 'What are you lot doing?'

So the Ferret said, 'We were cleaning the windows and then this silly bitch started poking us with an umbrella so I'll leave you to clean them yourself.'

I had to admire the Ferret. He might have had unusual tastes but he had style and he was cool under pressure.

Another time I had just him in this wardrobe and I swear to God there was no floor in the wardrobe. Someone had taken it up and there was this drop of about three or four miles with just a wooden slat over it. It didn't bother the Ferret.

I got the lighting right and the wireless playing and the bird was great. I couldn't stop and in the end I started doing it to the music on the wireless. And I remember saying to the bird, 'I hope they don't put a quickstep on or I'll drop dead'. And I heard the Ferret start laughing.

That was the only time he disgraced himself.

Otherwise he was as quiet as a mouse.

Sometimes when I couldn't get the bird into a room I'd take her outside and I'd be making it up against a tree or in the undergrowth somewhere and I'd see the Ferret crawling on his hands and knees to a good spot. He was always very quiet.

One day he brought another player with him who ruined things for everyone by being a noisy crawler.

Next morning I came downstairs and the Ferret had this player practising crawling across the hotel lounge. He said, 'You'll never be a good ferret if you don't listen to me.'

The Ferret was a bit special.

I'll tell you something, if he'd been as good at soccer he'd have been world class.

CHAPTER 8

The axiom that you have to be barmy to be the manager of a football team is only slightly exaggerated. It is not necessary to have a slate loose, but it certainly helps. It is an occupation of terrifying uncertainty, and the only promise it holds for the majority is a life of unremitting and unrewarding graft. There are more losers than winners in the game of football management.

However the job has given a few men special eminence and rewards – none more so than Sir Matt Busby. Busby became synonymous with Manchester United. During his twenty-three years at the club he built outstanding success from bare bones.

When he arrived at the club in 1945 the stadium was a heap of rubble. His first office was a nissen hut costing £30. Twenty-three years later he had made more than one million pounds for his club, had won unequalled success and reputation in the field of play and, perhaps more significantly, had survived while 600 of his fellow managers were being sacked. By 1969 he was the last remaining undisturbed manager of a first division club since 1945.

Busby's achievements were not altogether to be measured in terms of longevity and cups. He had brought a new style to football management in two particular and important areas. The first was in his relationship with his board of directors.

In the forties and fifties managers of soccer clubs were prey to the foibles of their boards of directors who were, in the main, well-meaning men, but ignorant of soccer. Often they interfered in matters of team selection, thereby making the manager's job impossible.

Len Shackleton, a great soccer player with an irrepressible sense of humour, summed up this period in his autobiography when

'I knew I was a good player and I knew I'd become well known –
but I wasn't prepared for what happened to me'

From digs with Mary
Fullaway to a new, £30000
'goldfish bowl' of a house

Everybody loves a winner: *Top :* George Best with Harold Wilson and (*above*) with Eva Haraldsted: 'You could say I fell in love with a pair of knockers'

Opposite : George Best, footballer, on the way to being Georgie, Superstar

Top: ' "Chopper" Harris, earning his money by following me round the park'

Above: Best brought back the verb 'to dribble' to the sportswriter's vocabulary

Top: The impudent player – Best caught the ball after Denis Law failed to make contact, and threw it into the net. But the 'goal' was disallowed

Above: Sent off for throwing mud at the referee

Above left: 'I love taking the piss out of players – like nutmegging them'

Above: Best and Law in training during the halcyon days

Left: With Bobby Charlton: 'When I first came to Old Trafford I thought he was a god . . . he became a bloody national institution'

under a heading, 'The average director's knowledge of soccer', he left a blank page.

Busby demanded, and received, a free hand from his directors. The running of the team was his concern and his alone. Louis Edwards, United's chairman and a firm friend and fan of Matt, says: 'He had a marvellous arrangement with us. I'd tell the board, "Matt's made up his mind but he's coming to us for advice".'

Busby's other achievement was to strike up a warm and helpful relationship with the press. It is true to say that the matter of press and public relations had a low priority rating at most soccer clubs, as it still has at some. These clubs work on the theory that the press crawl out of the woodwork every so often and should therefore be treated accordingly.

Busby would have none of this. His naturally avuncular style, his colossal charm, his remarkable memory for names (even if he couldn't always pronounce them properly) made him an ideal ambassador for his club. Indeed when United's fortunes and behaviour slumped badly from 1969 onwards, the club was treated with a kindness and understanding by press and public alike that was a direct result of Busby's personal public relations work over the years.

By the start of 1969 he was fulfilled. He had won the European Cup, he had been knighted. When they also made him a Freeman of Manchester it was simply officialdom's recognition that the city belonged to him.

Early in 1969 he announced he would give up his job as manager of Manchester United. He said at the time: 'I found that I was not spending enough time with the team and that is something you cannot afford. I feel it is time for someone in a track suit to take over the players out on the training pitch. As it is, United have become more than just a football club, they are now an institution.'

It was decided he would stay on as general manager with a team manager under him.

David Miller, then of the *Sunday Telegraph*, now of the *Daily Express*, summed up the situation perfectly when he said that Busby's successor would have 'both the best and the worst job in the world'.

Addressing Busby's successor (then not known) he went on:

You inherit not only an incomparable tradition, but a struggling team in an era when almost all opponents have some joyless antidote to excellence and individualism. Your job will be made much easier and more difficult because of the decision, not altogether wise in my opinion, that Sir Matt shall remain as general manager. You will be glad of his unrivalled experience, wisdom and diplomatic counsel, but inevitably you will be sometimes restricted and always overshadowed by his Olympian presence.

It will be that much harder to establish the respect and command in your own right which he has enjoyed.

It may well be, whatever your industry and leadership, whatever funds are at your disposal to acquire new players, that Manchester United are about to enter one of their leanest periods since the war. The great players, with the exception of Best, are slowing down, the existing youngsters seem to be short of former standards.

There never was a more prophetic article.

At the end of the 1969 season United finished eleventh, their lowest position since George Best joined the club. He was top scorer with nineteen goals but Busby knew, even then, that the star player was only operating at seventy-five per cent efficiency and was more often than not concentrating on matters not entirely connected with playing football.

Busby sensed that there was trouble ahead, and knew that whoever was appointed manager inherited in Best his most priceless asset and most testing problem.

In April 1969 Manchester United appointed Wilf McGuinness as chief coach with the prospect of becoming manager. The appointment was urged by Busby and sanctioned by the board. Since he was a boy McGuinness had been part of Busby's 'family' at Old Trafford and his appointment came as no surprise to those people who knew Busby's loyalty to his staff. However it caused a few knowing nods from those who believed that the club needed a stronger medicine.

Busby says: 'People said I was too loyal. How can you be too loyal? I chose McGuinness because I thought he was the best man for the job. I was wrong. It was a mistake.'

McGuinness was appointed chief coach in April 1969 and sacked from the job in December 1970. In those twenty months United went from crisis to crisis. Invariably George Best was at the eye of the storm, and not Wilf McGuinness nor Matt Busby nor all the heavenly hosts could have done a thing about it.

When Wilf McGuinness took over at Old Trafford George Best's career as an athlete was at the time in the balance. He was already a confirmed sybarite, a considerable drinker, a successful womanizer and a stop-out. He still trained hard, still pulled out the stops most Saturdays but he was finding it more and more difficult to define the line between his social activities and his career as an athlete.

His remarkable gifts remained intact. On song he was still the world's most exciting player displaying a range of gifts quite beyond the ken of other footballers, but it was becoming more difficult and it started to show.

It revealed itself in a growing petulance with authority which led to a series of unfortunate disputes with referees. The first occurred when United were playing Manchester City in a League Cup semi-final. Best, who had already been cautioned for kicking the ball away after a free kick had been awarded against him, knocked the ball out of the referee's hands as they were leaving the field. The incident was seen on television and the referee, Mr Jack Taylor, included it in his report to the Football Association.

Best was charged with bringing the game into disrepute, fined £100 and suspended for a month. It provoked this comment from David Meek of the *Manchester Evening News*:

It is impossible, of course, to defend the pointless petulant way the Irishman knocked the ball out of the referee's hand as they were leaving the field. But one can certainly question the severity of the punishment. . . . Best's conduct sheet over a long period is good. Two offences in foreign football and five cautions in domestic competitions is the sum total of his crimes in seven seasons of action in soccer's top grade.

Best is also one of the highest ranked players in the game and he has to endure a great deal of extremely hard tackling.

Best's reaction was childish but four weeks' suspension for what he

75

did seems to me to be out of all proportion. That length of punishment is surely meant for more serious offences involving either violence or persistent troublemaking . . . and Best is not guilty on either count.

Best was suspended for five matches, returned for a cup tie against Northampton Town and with typical panache scored six of United's eight goals. He was undoubtedly motivated by the letters he had received from 'fans' saying that United were better off without him. Typically he stuffed their abuse down their throats.

Three months later he was in trouble again. Playing for Ireland against Scotland in Belfast he was sent off for spitting and throwing mud at the referee. His next game was against England at Wembley where Best was booed every time he touched the ball. He repaid the insult with a performance of the highest quality.

Hugh McIlvanney wrote of the game:

The drone of disapproval that rose from the stands each time the dark, unmistakeably graceful figure moved onto the ball was essentially a comment on the juvenile show of ill temper which thrust Best back into conflict with the disciplinary authorities of the game the previous Saturday. There was something puritanical, smugly uncharitable about the Wembley crowd's reluctance to acknowledge that the bad boy was not so much top of the class but in a class of his own.

Yet while there is an obvious meanness of spirit about spectators who use their own moral arithmetic in an attempt to subtract from the genius of Best, it is a simple reality that unless he can rid his behaviour of the element of self indulgent provocation he is going to find more and more hostility on all sides.

Just before being sent off in Belfast, George Best became involved in another incident which did little to help his already tarnished image. He went to a nightclub with Pat Crerand and met his former fiancée, Eva Haraldsted, who was there with another boy friend. They teased each other by requesting certain records. Eva asked for 'I'm Leaving on a Jet Plane'. George replied with 'Get Back Where You Belong'.

Such a childish and almost comic exchange had serious consequences when a fight developed outside the club which led to

Crerand being charged with assaulting one man and committing grievous bodily harm on another.

It was alleged that Crerand broke Miss Haraldsted's friend's jaw with one blow and then struck another man. Crerand was cleared on both charges after the stipendiary magistrate had said that one of the prosecution witnesses had been irresponsible.

The public began to wonder what was wrong with George Best and typically he gave them an answer confessing to Miss Anthea Disney, an attractive feature writer for the then *Daily Sketch*: 'I've been playing badly for a couple of months now – due mostly to late nights and drink. I didn't think about it at the beginning. I just knew I was fed up with everything and everyone around me.

'So I went on going out every night and drinking when I should have been training.'

The confession explained a lot but pleased no one, particularly Mr Ernest Mudd Garnett. He was chairman of Bellair who paid Best £12000 to publicize their aftershave. Said Mr Garnett, 'We are trying to promote a clean-cut image and Mr Best is not helping. He will have to keep his nose clean in future, a lot of our dealers have a puritanical outlook on life.'

The Egg Marketing Board, which had used Best in a highly successful campaign to persuade people to eat more eggs, was altogether more sanguine. A spokesman said, 'His moral affairs are not our concern. Our answer would be he didn't have an egg for breakfast the day he threw mud at the ref.'

Sir Matt Busby and Wilf McGuinness were less than delighted with Best's public confessional. Both had realized what was going on but had hoped to keep the matter within the club, to sort the player out in private instead of having his problems strung out for everyone to see.

'I'll straighten him out if it's the last thing I do,' Busby said. McGuinness kept his counsel. His first season as coach had not been altogether unsuccessful. His team had reached the semi-final of the Cup, it had finished eighth in the League and Best, for all his problems, was once more top scorer with twenty-five goals.

Perhaps next season might be better.

You could only hope.

In fact there wasn't any.
George Best saw to that.

*   *   *

GEORGE'S STORY

When Matt gave up his job as manager he said he wanted a younger
man to take over, a track-suit manager who could train with the
players. Wilf McGuinness was a nice fella and he used to do his
training by chasing after me. I suppose I led him a bit of a dance
at times but at least I didn't rubbish him like one or two of our
players did.

My only criticism of Wilf would be that he didn't get enough
sleep when we were away from home. In fact he used to spend all
his time prowling up and down outside my bedroom door just in
case I nipped out for a quick poke. Sometimes he won and sometimes he lost. I will tell you about one of each.

First the time when he got two points. We were down in London
on a Friday night playing Chelsea the next afternoon. Nights like
that the lads normally go to the pictures then get an early night.
Usually I went with them but this night I felt like a bit of romance.
Moreover I fancied a mystery.

I used to get a few letters and phone calls from birds saying,
'When you're in town, call me'. I never did because blind dates are
always disastrous. Anyway this time I broke my rule and phoned
up a bird who was always calling me. She had a voice that gave me
a hard and I thought she had to be good news.

Anyway I called round to see her and when she opened the door
I knew I had made a terrible mistake. A dog, a real ugly dog. Anyway she takes me into her front room, gives me a drink and says
she is going to take a bath so would I nip along in a minute and
scrub her back. I told her I had to phone my stockbroker first,
then as soon as she had left the room I fucked off out of the house
and ran down the road .

Now I'm lumbered, aren't I? The lads are at the cinema, I'm as
randy as hell and I'm stuck in the middle of bloody London with
nowhere to go. So I headed for an Italian restaurant I knew and

had a steak with the owner. I was sitting there, facing the door, like I always do to spot the talent, when this darling bird walked by.

My friend, the owner, chased after her and brought her back. She was an American visiting London and said her name was Susanna. She wasn't doing anything in particular so I asked her to have a drink with me. She was a bloody marvellous looking chick and she didn't know me from a hole in the head, or so she said.

Now I have to start plotting how to pull her because things are difficult. First she hasn't got a flat so that means I have to take her back to the hotel. It has to be my hotel because I have to be tucked in by the manager otherwise he goes bloody spare.

After a while I asked Susanna where she was staying and she said she had planned to stay with a friend but there had been some confusion. I said she ought to stay at our hotel and she said O.K. but she had to see someone first so she'd come round later. I rang up the hotel and told them Susanna would be staying and that she was a journalist doing a story about me.

It wasn't the first time I'd pulled that stroke. In fact the staff at that hotel must be under the impression that Fleet Street is full of birds who look like Miss Universe.

So I went back to the hotel in good time, saw Wilf, said 'Good night, boss', like a well behaved athlete and went to bed.

When I went out for the evening I was feeling randy, now I am feeling exceedingly randy. I lay on my bed waiting for the phone call from Susanna saying she had arrived at the hotel. Eleven o'clock, nothing. Midnight, nothing. I'm just beginning to curse her, thinking she had given me the elbow when the phone went. It was Susanna saying she was in her room. I tell her I am coming up to tuck her in.

It is now about one o'clock and the rest of the players are asleep, dreaming about tomorrow's game. I am thinking about something entirely different. Although the players are in bed, I am not so sure about Wilf McGuinness. He is a nice man, and I got on very well with him, but he had a suspicious mind and I don't think he trusted me. So I opened the door gently and looked up and down the corridor but there is no sign of him.

In situations like this I always use the fire escape because you don't know who you will bump into in a lift. So I headed down the corridor for the fire escape which is through two swing doors. I am just opening the swing doors, one flight away from paradise, when I see Wilf standing with his back to me looking out of the window. I froze, let the door close gently and then ran back down the corridor like a fucking rocket. He must have seen me because when I got into my room and locked it I heard someone come and gently try the door handle.

It's now about 1.30 a.m. so I ring Susanna and say I've been a bit delayed ringing my sister in Miami but hang about and I'll be up. I waited until about 2 a.m. then I opened the door and Wilf McGuinness is outside pacing up and down like a fucking guardsman.

Three o'clock I have another look and he's still there. I rang the bird up and told her the truth. I told her I couldn't get out of my room because the manager is patrolling outside. She obviously didn't understand because she started laughing. I told her not to worry because I would be up first thing in the morning.

I put my alarm on for 8 a.m. but I can't sleep for thinking about this lovely bird upstairs. At eight I'm out of bed like a shot, peer outside and Wilf has finally gone to bed.

I dash up the stairs, get into Susanna's room, and what happens? Nothing. She doesn't want to know. All that crap about let's not rush it and all that poloney. So there I am, the world's greatest footballer a few hours from an important game with eyes like pissoles in the snow.

What is more I am reckoned to be one of Britain's sexiest men and I haven't had a fuck. I was in a right foul mood. Just before the game starts Wilf says to me, 'Go out, George, and do it for me'. I didn't tell him what I was thinking.

Wilf won that one, but he lost another in fairly spectacular fashion. I always fancied having a quick fuck before a game. I mean minutes before, not the night before. I fancied the dressing room at Wembley just before a cup final. Anyway, I've never believed all that bollocks about it sapping your strength. It never did me any harm, except this once I'm going to tell you about.

We were playing in a semi-final and the club had sent us away for a few days to rest up in this hotel. I used to die of boredom in those places. The rest of the lads liked it because they could get away from the wife for a while and play golf all the time. I didn't play golf, it interfered with my sex life.

Anyway we are stuck in this bloody place and the only thing that keeps me from going mad is this bird who every day comes and sits at the bar or in the lounge and reads a book. I tried to start a conversation with her but nothing doing. I used to keep looking across at her just for a tiny reaction, but she never blinked.

It was like that for the three days we were there. Anyway on the last day we were playing in the evening in the semi-final and normally I would sleep in the afternoon before a big game. This time I couldn't sleep. I kept thinking about the bird and she worried me.

I went downstairs and she was coming upstairs. She spoke to me. She said she didn't like to bother me before but because this was our last day at the hotel could she bother me for an autograph for her daughter. I said she could have an autograph if I could buy her a drink. So we went in the bar and Wilf came in. He didn't say anything but he kept watching us. So I asked her to come to the lounge to watch television. Wilf came in after us and sat with one eye on the box and one eye on us.

There is now about three hours to kick off and I'm wondering just how I am going to get this bird into bed. I just can't say, 'Excuse me, can we go to your room and have a quick fuck because I'm playing football in three hours' time'. I said to her, 'Look, that man over there keeps looking at us. Can we go to your room to watch television?' And she agreed.

We went upstairs into her room and I didn't start any action straightaway because I expected Wilf to come knocking any minute. After about half an hour he hadn't shown so I thought I had the all clear. There was about two hours left before kick-off which was more than ample time to deal with the young lady. I had just started work, just got me shirt and pants off when the bloody door opens and Wilf walks in.

He's as mad as bloody hell and he's got the pass key in his hand

He orders me out of the room and there I am walking down the corridor escorted by my boss in my bloody underwear with my gear under my arm like I've been bloody arrested or something.

Wilf is flaming mad. I've never seen a bloke so angry. He's telling me to get to my room and change because the bus is due in half an hour and he's never heard of anything like it in all his life. Ninety minutes before a semi-final and someone wants a fuck.

Anyway he storms off downstairs leaving me to get to my room. I stood at the top of the stairs and heard him go in the bar and order a large whisky. He must have been in a terrible state because he didn't even drink whisky. I waited for a minute then instead of going to my room I went back to see the bird.

She was still there where I left her, still ready and willing. I apologized for Wilf and said he always got a bit het up before a big game. Then I clambered into bed and made love to her. I had to be fairly quick about it because the team bus was due very shortly. It was very nice anyway and when I had finished I said, 'Excuse me, I have to go now to play in the semi-final'.

She said she understood. I remember as I left she was lying there on the bed with nothing on and I picked up a chiffon scarf and dropped it over her like I was covering it up until I got back. I did some daft things sometimes.

Anyway I didn't go back. I went on the team bus to play Leeds in the semi-final. I played like a big wanker. Once I was clean through with the ball and I fell over it. I lay there and buried my head in the mud. The crowd gave me the bird but they didn't know what I was thinking.

Anyway we lost and I played badly. I don't think it had anything to do with the woman in the hotel. I just felt poorly at the time.

That was one time when Wilf didn't stop me.

I felt sorry when Wilf left.

He was a bloody nuisance when it came to stopping me birding, but when he went, although it was easier, it wasn't half so much fun.

CHAPTER 9

By December 1970, after twenty months on trial as chief coach, Wilf McGuinness was relieved of his job. The team was fifth from the bottom of the first division and the directors, worried about the prospect of relegation, asked Busby to assume command.

McGuinness had, in fact, done quite a good job for the club under exceedingly difficult circumstances. It is no secret that several of the players who had grown up shoulder to shoulder with McGuinness during his career at Old Trafford resented taking orders from him when he was appointed to authority. Similarly McGuinness found it difficult to assume command of people like Bobby Charlton and Denis Law whose maturity and glamour perhaps required handling by an older, more experienced man.

But McGuinness didn't lack courage and while it could be argued that Busby at the end of his initial reign refused to see the faults in his team, McGuinness boldly pointed the way. He dropped old established players like Foulkes and Crerand. He dared to leave out the idols like Law and Charlton. In his first season United finished a respectable eighth in the League and in 1970 lost to Leeds in the semi-final of the FA Cup.

In his book *In My Way* Sir Matt Busby wonders what McGuinness's future might have been had United beaten Leeds in the semi-final and reached Wembley. McGuinness, who, for a time, managed a club in Greece, must wonder about that too and contemplate what might have been had not his greatest player done his pre-match training in bed.

Reluctantly Busby resumed control of his team and immediately encountered a major problem with George Best.

In January 1971 Best was due to appear before an FA Disciplinary Commission after having acquired three cautions for misconduct on the field in a period of twelve months. He arranged to travel with Sir Matt to London but missed the train. He arrived three hours late, was fined £250 and given a six-week suspended sentence.

Much was made of Best's lateness and also the fact that the fine was the highest ever imposed on an individual. Miss Jean Rook, then of the *Daily Sketch*, now of the *Daily Express*, wrote in her inimitable style: 'Isn't it time somebody told George Best he's getting far too big for his football boots? Or am I the only ex-fan who's sick of watching young twinkle ankles treating other people like they were the ball?

'George, you're gorgeous, nobody doubts it. Mr Fab Feet himself. The sexiest thing that ever slid inside a soccer shirt two sizes too tight. You're also becoming a great big-headed, baby-faced bore. Grow up and belt up, why don't you? Just switch it off a bit, eh?'

Needless to say Mr Best ignored Miss Rook's advice. Four days after appearing before the Commission he missed the train taking his team to London to play Chelsea. He came on a later train to spend a weekend with actress Sinead Cusack. If Best and Miss Cusack had hoped for a quiet weekend, alone together, they acutely misjudged the media's interest in everything George Best did.

In fact the couple spent three days besieged in Miss Cusack's flat, unable to get out through the encircling ring of camera crews and photographers who trained their equipment on Miss Cusack's lace curtains. The journalists worked in shifts in case George Best did a moonlight flit.

Looking back at it later, Sir Matt Busby said, 'I don't think any other single thing that happened to the boy brought home to me his problem. All right, he had been silly and irresponsible. But for three days and nights he was front page and back page news. Cameras watched all night for him. He was on television news. I sat there and wondered how he was to survive it all.'

Best's progress in Miss Cusack's flat, or lack of it, was reported on television and radio with bulletins at regular intervals in the manner of royal illnesses.

As the news of his whereabouts spread through the land the mob of journalists outside Miss Cusack's flat was augmented by young autograph hunters. At one time they gained entrance to the building and were ejected by the police along with two television crews.

The children started by shouting, 'We want Georgie', or 'Come out, Georgie'. When their hero showed no sign of appearing the children changed their mood. 'Georgie Best is on the nest', they chanted.

Eventually Best was rescued from his predicament by two friends from Manchester who drove down to London and, with police help, smuggled him back to Manchester. He said he wanted a 'showdown' with Busby and he got it. But it was an anti-climax. The club suspended him for two weeks and Busby gave the player a heart-to-heart.

Even allowing for Busby's renowned patience with, and understanding of, soccer players, there is little doubt that had George Best been less than the world's best player and Manchester's one hope of keeping afloat, he would have been dismissed in the most decisive fashion.

Best apologized to Busby in private and then repeated the apology for the benefit of waiting journalists. In the meantime the leader writers of *The Guardian* and *The Times*, not hitherto renowned for their interest in footballers, devoted their attention to George Best.

The Times, under a leader headed 'The Price of Indiscipline', discussed the lack of discipline on the field of play and then stated:

Over the past few days, of course, it is indiscipline off the field of play which has done more to damage the game's reputation. The successful player can now become a wealthy man quite quickly. Much of his money is likely to come from businesses he may run or be associated with, or products he may sponsor. He may get caught up in the show business whirl with all the opportunities and temptations that involves. This is liable to make it harder for the player to retain his sense of proportion and enthusiasm for the game and for the club to exert its control over the player.

The club may have launched him but once he is in orbit as a star he is no longer dependent upon it for his wealth or his fame. It is the club which in many cases may be doubtful if it can do without him.

To the outside observer the suspension of a fortnight imposed by

Manchester United on George Best must seem a remarkably lenient punishment for an episode which has so harmed the reputation of the game, the club and the player. Such leniency may be understandable, and it may be justified in individual cases by circumstances of which the outside observer is not aware. But in the long run football will retain its present hold over the general public only if nothing so damages any great sport over a period of time as for attention to be diverted consistently away from the game itself to the storms and tempests on the fringe.

The Guardian, under the heading 'Footballer of the Week', gave the issue a much more sidelong glance:

Now that famed soccer idol George (I was wrong) Best has made his peace with doyen manager (We start from scratch again) Busby, what are we to make of Monday's Islington flat drama and business associate Malcolm Mooney's eleventh hour M1 car dash? Before these incidents sink again into the obscurity from which they never should have emerged, let us wring what agony remains from stormy petrel Best's tiff with award winning United's world renowned Sir (Mr Football) Matt.

Inquirers at the twenty-three year old player's £35 000 Bramhall, Cheshire, dream house got a brusque 'No comment' late last night when they asked whether the Babe's ebullient outside left had missed three London bound expresses accidentally or on purpose. The boutique owning soccer wizard was not available to reporters. Meanwhile we can reveal that blonde Irish actor's daughter Sinead (say Shin-aid) Cusack was at dinner with successful Manchester businessman Best on Sunday night prior to the practice session at Manchester United's The Cliff training ground where Best's dramatic Monday morning non-appearance led stern-faced Sir Matt to invoke a two week suspension of the star. Later 'Guardian' reader Sinead took in milk from the crowd thronged doorstep of her Noel Road, Islington, flat. '(Bearded International) George (Best) is very upset', confided Miss Cusack (22).

Best (I've apologised) sat yesterday at the right of 61-year-old Freeman of Manchester Sir Matt and said: 'It was completely wrong and I know it'. Thus ended a seven day saga culminating in the 'Pimpernel' Ulsterman's police escorted departure from the flat of girl friend Sinead in a white Jaguar. 'Indiscipline', reproved London's prestigious Thomson owned 'Times' newspaper. 'Tedium', says the (former Manchester) Guardian.

Sir Matt Busby could be forgiven if he didn't even smile at *The Guardian*'s attempt at satire. He was preoccupied finding yet another successor to himself. In defence of the suggestion that he was too lenient with Best, Busby says, 'What were we to do, shoot him? I always looked for a cure with George. It would have been easy to have transferred him but that wasn't the answer. Special rules for George? I suppose so, but only in the sense that he was a special player. I mean you make it different once you say someone is a good player and the man next to him is a genius. George is a genius.'

In early 1971 Manchester appointed Frank O'Farrell as the new manager. O'Farrell, formerly manager at Leicester, brought Malcolm Musgrove with him as his coach. The club appointed Sir Matt Busby a director. Sir Matt reiterated his intention to leave the running of the club to the manager.

There was money available for new players. The new manager had a good record and seemed ideal for the job. The one problem was George Best. 'Any manager would love a problem like that', said Sir Matt.

He was wrong. George Best was to bring down Frank O'Farrell. The club was to drop to its lowest ever depths. Not only was it to lose its status in the first division, it was to lost its reputation as an institution.

People always believed that no matter what happened United would react with style. In fact when the red alert sounded they behaved like any other club in trouble. Arthur Hopcraft, an affectionate observer of United's affairs over ten years, wrote:

'The events at Old Trafford between the summer of 1969 and the close of 1972 had a distressing shabbiness. Wilf McGuinness, a product of the famous Busby nursery of the 1950s, was callously given the responsibility of managing the players while denied convincing authority because Sir Matt stayed in his old office, an intimidating grey eminence called "General Manager". When McGuinness failed, inevitably, he was humiliated by being returned to the reserve team on transfer (he left the club later) and Sir Matt took the reins again. A new manager, Frank O'Farrell, lasted eighteen months before the cumulative hindrances of acrimony in the dressing room, disfavour in the newspapers and the defection of George Best to the Never Never Land unfitted him for the job in the eyes of the Directors, of whom Sir Matt was now one. It was a sorry tale of equivocation and disavowal.'

Frank O'Farrell arrived in Manchester and George Best flew away to Spain and the sun leaving behind all thoughts of disciplinary committees, journalists and Sinead Cusack.

There were other joys to taste – and bigger crises ahead than anyone had dreamed of.

* * *

GEORGE'S STORY

Some journalist once asked me how many girls I'd had. I said a thousand, but I ought to have said, 'Who's counting?' All that talk about women weakening an athlete is a load of bollocks. I read an article once which said a man ran a mile in under four minutes an hour after having sex. Well, that doesn't prove anything either. I mean it doesn't follow that he ran a sub-four-minute mile because he had sex but it does show that being with a woman doesn't knacker you like it's supposed to.

All that having sex did for me was make me want more.

People think I'm some sort of bloody sex maniac or something but I'm just normal. The only difference with me is (or was) that instead of being a normal young man with healthy appetites I was an abnormal young man with very healthy appetites.

I mean abnormal in the sense that I was super fit. Only an athlete will know what it's like to be as fit as I was, to feel like you could knock down buildings or make love all night.

It used to amuse me when I was in trouble with the club, the press used to say, 'George Best looking overweight and unfit'. Cheeky sods. I mean take a look at your average journalist and I'll show you a drink-sodden, overweight man who couldn't make it with Racquel Welch.

Even nowadays when I'm only a quarter as fit as I used to be I'm still fitter than your average person.

If you want the secret of my success with women – ignoring the fact that I'm George Best which always helps – then don't smoke, don't take drugs and don't be too particular. The last piece of advice is very important because one or two ladies of my acquaintance would have had a bad time in a beauty contest but they remain in my mind a long time after I've forgotten some of the lookers.

Also to be successful with ladies you must not make rules – like some people I know won't sleep with their friends' wives. Some won't sleep with married women, others don't like black girls, or Jewesses, or girls with big knockers or bandy legs. You shouldn't make rules about women because if they are willing they are worth while no matter who or what they are.

My favourite women have been the ones with a certain style. There was one I remember who was married and very rich and wherever I went she used to send her chauffeur to meet me. So I'd be walking down the platform at Euston with the team or arriving at Manchester Airport and there would be this geezer in a bottle-green uniform waiting for me. She used to give me a white box with a ribbon round it and in the box was a red rose. That's style.

Then there was another girl I met in Spain, a German bird who used to come on the beach every day with this old fella. She never looked at anyone else. In the end I managed to get chatting to her except she didn't speak English – nor do I if it comes to that.

Anyway I brought a phrase book with me and we began to communicate. She had to go home with the old sod but I persuaded her to return without him. She came to Majorca and stayed with me but I got fed up after a couple of days. It was a right bloody drag having to use the phrase book every time you wanted to say, 'Pass the salt', or, 'Do you feel sleepy?'

Anyway one night I went out without her and came back with another girl. The German bird's in bed asleep so I take this other girl into the spare bedroom and give her one. Next morning the German bird wakes me up. She's fully dressed for an aeroplane so she's obviously on her way home.

I sat up in bed and she beckoned me forward with her finger. I leaned forward thinking she's going to kiss me good-bye and she goes whack straight on the chin end. Bloody well knocked me out.

89

When I came round she's gone but there's her wrist watch round my ankle with a little note saying it's to pay for the tickets I sent her to come to Majorca. That was a class bird.

Birds kept me sane. I know a lot of people think the opposite but they are wrong. Whenever things got too tough, whenever I got depressed because the team was playing bad and I couldn't take all the limelight and wanted to get away I used to find myself a bird.

That's what happened with Sinead. She's one of the few girls I really liked – and still do. Like I said before the majority of birds wanted me just because I was George Best, but Sinead was different. She didn't need that kind of publicity.

I met her on a talk show in Dublin and couldn't get her out of my mind. She gave me a number to ring and I did so and I heard a man shout in the background, 'Tell him to fuck off'.

Promising beginning.

Anyway we got together when we were both back in England and I grew very fond of her. We kept it quiet for a while because she didn't want the publicity and I needed it like a broken leg.

Anyway one day I'm in London and going to take Sinead out to dinner when this reporter comes up to me and says, 'I hear you're going out with Sinead Cusack'. So I told the guy it was nonsense.

He said he was going to follow me all round London because he didn't believe me. So, because I didn't want him sitting between Sinead and myself in the restaurant, I told him what the score was.

I said there was no romance. I said I was going to take her for dinner and that was all and I said that he mustn't use a word because she had a boy friend (the voice on the phone) and it wouldn't be fair. He left me with the impression that he had agreed.

Yet, two days later and it's front page in his lousy paper and all that crap. They'd even put in a quote from me saying that I felt it wasn't fair because she already had a boy friend.

Sinead was bloody angry. She rang me up and called me all the names. I managed to persuade her that I had nothing to do with the story and she eventually believed me, so we got together.

I needed those three days with her in London. I had just had the disciplinary commission, the papers had given me some bloody stick, the team was rubbish and I needed somewhere to go, someone to talk to. I talked to Sinead all the time I stayed with her and felt a lot better after.

It was a daft bloody scene though. All the press and television and the kids outside. Sinead and I just sat there and watched the story on television news. It was unreal watching pictures on telly of the flat you were sitting in. It was like acting a play in a packed theatre without the curtain going up.

It did me good those few days even though it showed to Sinead and myself just how bloody impossible it was for us to have a proper relationship together.

I remember one night we managed to slip out without the press noticing. We went for a meal and returned at four in the morning. It was a bit misty and as we approached Sinead's flat we heard this guy following and whistling 'A Foggy Day in London Town'. He caught up with us and said he was a journalist and he'd been waiting all night to catch us and all that old bollocks. We got to the flat and he said, 'Come on, George, I've waited all this time, now what about a quote?'

I said, 'I'll give you a quote. Rearrange the following two words to make a well-known phrase or saying, "Off fuck" ' and I slammed the door in his face.

I hated the press. They used to tell such bloody great lies about me. When I finally gave the game up they all wrote I was drinking a bottle of scotch a day. Everyone knows I'm a vodka drinker.

One journalist once asked Malcolm Wagner, a great friend of mine, what he liked about me. Malcolm said I had a great sense of humour. The guy said, 'Tell me something funny he said'. Malcolm said he couldn't off hand. It appears in the paper, 'Mr Wagner said George Best had a sense of humour but was unable to recall anything funny he had said or done'.

Now that is not nice.

It hurts.

Anyway girls like Sinead were the cure for all that. She is one of the few I really liked. Funny though, while I was going out with her I was bothered about one thing, that voice on the phone when I rang her in Dublin, the one saying, 'Tell him to fuck off'.

One morning at about 4 a.m. I rang the number and the bloke answered.

'Hello,' he said.

'And you fuck off too,' I said and put the phone down.

I definitely felt a lot better.

Looking back at the girls with this style I was talking about I remember another one, whose name I won't mention because she's married. She is very well known and made a name in a television series and I met her when she was in Manchester working. At the time Frank O'Farrell was the manager and I was going through one of my depressions.

I met her on Friday, went back to her flat and didn't get up till the following Monday. Three days just making love and eating while everybody outside went bloody spare trying to find me.

Eventually I had to go back and face the music so I went to see Frank and he said, 'What are we going to tell the press?' So I said, 'Tell them I was in bed with a touch of flu'.

So next day every paper has the headline, 'Best Returns. Spent weekend in bed with touch of the flu'.

That afternoon I get a telegram. It read:

> 'Roses are red,
> Violets are blue,
> I've never been called
> A touch of the flu.'

And she signed it.

That girl had a lot of style.

A pity she was married and I'm daft as a brush.

CHAPTER 10

For a while, under Frank O'Farrell, George Best and Manchester United were newly weds, blissful and charged with unconcerned optimism. Best at twenty-five was approaching new peaks of virtuosity. He was blending experience with his unequalled gifts and the overall maturity of his play was in perfect unison with the odd, incredible moments of unpredictable genius that made him the biggest box office attraction in British soccer.

A holiday in Spain, a break from the game, a minor truce with alcohol and late nights and the excitement of a team under new management had given Best a new purpose.

It lasted only half a season during which time Best scored fourteen goals and Manchester United were at the top of the first division.

Then, almost a year after his talk with Busby, Best initiated a series of events that were to lead eventually to his own personal downfall and disaster for his club.

His troubles started when he was told he would be shot while playing for Manchester United at Newcastle. The threat came from a man claiming he was speaking on behalf of the IRA.

For some time Best, a Belfast Protestant whose parents live in that benighted city, had been the subject of abusive letters and telephone calls. There were rumours that he had given £3000 to the Protestant leader, Rev. Ian Paisley. They were not true but, as Best remarked, 'It's the kind of lie that can get you shot'.

As the troubles in Ireland worsened so the more the player, the club and the police were inclined to believe the threats. Best was told if he went to Ireland to play an international game in Belfast he would not return. A letter signed by 'The Striker' threatened a knife in the back and said, 'Next time you will miss your own biggest headline'.

Manchester United refused Best permission to travel to Belfast and after the threat to his life at Newcastle the police kept his house under surveillance.

At Newcastle he was flanked by two detectives who never left him. His meals were sent to his room and he ate in the presence of the detectives.

About forty police mingled with the crowd during the game and in spite of all the worry and the pressure Best played well and scored a goal.

He said: 'I never stopped moving on the field. I had the daft idea that it's difficult to hit a moving target. Even when the game was held up for somebody injured or the like I never stopped moving about. When I scored the goal I kept moving. I kidded our players it was the only time I had ever scored without the rest of the team coming and congratulating me. I was really frightened, I don't mind admitting, and when I scored the goal I was hoping they'd take me off the field – but they didn't.'

After the game the police gave the team coach an escort of two cars for the drive back to Manchester.

A week later a woman living near George Best's house was approached by two men who wanted his address. She told the police that when she looked out of the window after the departing men one appeared to be carrying a gun.

From then on the stream of fans to Best's front door was supplemented by two-hourly visits from the police to check he was all right.

From that moment Best's form declined in spectacular fashion. Needless to say the team were soon struggling. He went back to the destructive routine of drinking and late nights and finally, after missing training for a week, flew off to London to spend a much publicized weekend with his current girl friend, Miss Great Britain, Carolyn Moore.

The press speculated on marriage. Miss Moore denied it, and for a while attracted the kind of publicity that delighted the various companies who had hired a beauty queen and found themselves with the woman who might become Mrs George Best.

Lyons, the ice cream firm, were the first to glean the benefits of the situation. They had booked Miss Moore as their Lyons Maid to sit in state at the hideously titled Hotelympia, the catering industry's biennial exhibition in London.

How much extra ice cream Miss Moore sold because of her new found fame is not known but she certainly became the centre of attraction, stealing the limelight from a giant edible steamroller made entirely of chocolate, and appearing for television interviews about her love life wearing a Lyons Maid sash.

The speculation about George Best's love life led Miss Eva Haraldsted to write in *The People* a heart-rending account of their time together called 'George Best the lover'.

In the article Miss Haraldsted told an eager world that they had a row in a Chinese restaurant because he ate spare ribs with his fingers and she didn't think that was very nice. But when they made up she was so happy she cried and the mascara ran down George's shirt front.

He wore it for the next two days.

After a few hundred words of breathtaking banality Miss Haraldsted concluded: 'But of this I am sure, it is better to have loved and lost than never to have loved at all'. To which she might have added that if you have to love and lose you might as well love George Best because, in fact, you gain, particularly if you sell your story to the British press.

Frank O'Farrell, in the meantime, became the latest manager to try and sort out George Best.

Again, like Busby and McGuinness before him, he found himself facing a situation complicated only by the fact that the player on the mat was George Best, not Joe Bloggs. Bloggs would have been given a transfer and sent packing but O'Farrell, as a manager trying to get results, knew that Best was the man who could do the job for him, provided he could straighten him out.

O'Farrell fined Best, ordered him to do special training and told him he must go back to Mrs Fullaway's. Best paid the £300 fine without missing it, lapped up the special training because he needed it and ignored the order about going back to Mrs Fullaway's.

95

The newpapers seemed generally agreed that Best had been treated leniently, all except the *Morning Star* which stated:

'To order a twenty-five-year-old man to move out of his own house and to return to his digs, like some erring schoolboy, is an intolerable intrusion of privacy.

'O'Farrell said Best would be ordered to live in lodgings until the end of the season. "This is in his own interests so that he can have more supervision when he is away from the club."

'Perhaps George Best should get in touch with the Governor of Strangeways prison. He would get plenty of supervision there.'

The *Daily Mail* referred Best's problems to a psychiatrist. He reported:

'Typical for a star so removed from reality, Mr Best has built for himself a god-complex house. Tycoons build them for themselves just as did Roman emperors.

'Mr Best, inside a ten foot high fence and with smoked glass windows, might as well be in a castle in Spain.

'It is ex-directory, inaccessible. Rarely does the emperor/god entertain there. If he has a business appointment or lunches, they take place in restaurants.

'Guests admitted to the god-mansion are to recognize how favoured they are. The car will be full of gadgets – a god chariot.'

One day in May at 5 a.m. a very drunk emperor/god clambered into his god-chariot and after colliding with several other ordinary chariots on the way, arrived at his god-complex house. From there he took a taxi to the airport and flew to Spain. He booked into the Skol Hotel in Marbella and waited for the world to catch up with him.

When the press arrived he locked himself in a bedroom and spent the time drinking and reading the bits of paper that were shoved under his door. These contained offers from newspapers for his life story.

He chose the *Sunday Mirror* who paid him £5000. In the article Best said he had finished with football for good. He described himself as a physical and mental wreck in danger of drinking himself stupid. The *Mirror* reporters told their readers that Best's eyes brimmed with tears as he told his tale.

Best confessed in the article that he was near a mental break-down.

Back in Britain attitudes to Best's predicament varied. Bernard Manning, a north country comedian, said on television: 'Whoever heard of an Irishman having a mental breakdown?'

Ken Stanley, on holiday in Stratford-upon-Avon, read the news and said, 'Bloody hell'. It was the first he knew of it.

Carolyn Moore said she was surprised, and was never heard of again.

The Best saga was discussed in the House of Commons. On 24 May 1972, there appeared on the order paper between backbench motions about disabled workers and compensations for mining subsidence a cheeky quotation from Voltaire, 'The Best is the enemy of the good'.

It was put there by Mr Michael Clark Hutchinson, Conservative MP for Edinburgh. He was criticized by the Labour MP James Johnson who called it 'shameful' and 'disturbing' that United's star should be so treated.

'There is no doubt whatever of the imputation of this particular wording,' said Mr Johnson. 'Many of us have our own views about this young man, George Best. But this debases the coinage of the order paper. This is a calculated insult to a young man who can't hit back.'

Mr Clark Hutchinson replied that he was a Heart of Midlothian supporter. 'It may be reported as a bit of Celtic humour and I shall do my best not to offend in the future', he said.

He was congratulated by Sir Robert Carey, a Conservative MP who said he represented a Manchester constituency and supported Manchester United.

The Speaker, Mr Selwyn Lloyd, refused to do anything about the motion saying that censorship by him would be very disagreeable.

Others were less inclined to see the humour of the situation.

Just before running away to Spain Best had signed a contract for menswear with a Yorkshire textile company and part of the advertising campaign was a personal recorded message from Best which you could get by phoning a Halifax number.

The message said, 'I am on your side and I am sure I will be able to score for you again'. The magazine also said, 'The Best salesman you've ever had'. The slogan was beginning to look distinctly optimistic.

When Best announced his retirement the shares of the company that had purchased his name for more than £25 000 dropped from 137p to 114p. The company insisted: 'Best's personal affairs will not affect his business activities'.

The business world seemed to console itself with the view that any publicity was better than none at all. One public relations man said at the time, 'Best's brand awareness has never been so high'.

In six months' time he was made to eat his words because George Best's retirement from football was only the beginning of the end.

For himself and a few others besides.

*   *   *

GEORGE'S STORY

It's too easy to say I finished with football because I drank too much and did not behave like a professional sportsman. The question remains – why? I first started thinking seriously about United and myself after we won the European Cup. I think we were one of the worst teams to win it. We certainly weren't a good side and we needed new players badly. Bobby and Denis weren't getting any younger. Paddy wouldn't last forever. It didn't bother me, it just worried me.

Also I got pissed off because I thought United should have built a team round me and not Bobby Charlton. I think that after the European Cup Matt should have called me in and said he was going to build a great team round me. But he didn't and things just started to deteriorate.

After the European Cup I knew and everyone knew I was one of the greatest players in the world and yet I was playing at international level with a bad team and at club level with a side which could only go downhill. Also, to me, the training at United was boring, a fucking joke, as far as I was concerned.

I decided to tell Matt about it, get it off my chest. It was weeks before I plucked up courage. I used to rehearse what I was going to say because I wasn't talking to a nig-nog. I was talking to one of the greatest managers of all time. So eventually I went to see him.

I told him everything that I thought was wrong, that they were building the team round the wrong player, that the training was boring, that there were no new young players coming through. He sat and listened and then he gave me a right bollocking. He said I wasn't telling him the truth and that the things wrong at the club were really my own doing, my drinking and all that.

It knocked me back a bit because I was telling him the truth and trying to say that all the drinking was due to the fact that I was bored and couldn't see the future.

Anyway I left his office and thought, 'Bollocks'. I couldn't see us getting a team together for another six or seven years when I'd be nearing thirty and I couldn't imagine those years of waiting. I didn't want to leave United because there wasn't another club I wanted to go to so I was dropped.

There were other things too. I was worried by what was happening at home. I'd not seen Mum and Dad as much as I ought to have done and they used to worry about me. They'd read some crap in the paper about me and they'd worry. It made them quite ill. Mum would go out and she'd hear people say things about me and it got so she stayed in rather than go out. That used to make me so bloody angry.

But I was really angry with myself because I knew I was responsible. I knew that I ought to have gone and seen them more and given them more attention but somehow there was never enough time. I mean I'd send them money and things when they needed it but what they needed most was me being there and I wasn't able to give them that.

I still tried though on the park. After some games I'd be so knackered that my eyes were ringed black with exhaustion. I used to sit in the dressing room and not be able to move at all. I'd sit there for four hours sometimes, too tired to drink a cup of tea. If someone had said 'I'll give you a pill and you'll die' I'd have taken it.

Wilf McGuinness and Frank O'Farrell were both great at that time. They'd come up and say, 'You did your bit today. Hang about, do your bit and I'll sort the rest out.' But how long can you last?

That's another thing, after Matt retired we had Wilf and Frank in quick succession. But we didn't want managers, we needed players. Managers don't win or lose games, it's the players on the pitch who do that.

I liked both Wilf and Frank. I felt sorry for Wilf. He didn't have a bloody chance. Some of the players resented him. Frank always gave me a fair deal. In fact he was the only manager who gave me a rise. I went in one day and he said, 'I've been looking at the wages we pay and there are a couple of players getting more than you. I'm going to remedy that.' He did. He upped me from £170 a week to £225 which is what Bobby and Denis were getting.

The fact is I never cared about the bloody contract, all I wanted to get straight was the football. I felt I couldn't wait.

I used to watch Denis at the end of his career and think, 'I hope he doesn't stay too long. I hope he retires at the top.' He was such a great player that I couldn't bear the thought of some father bringing his son to see Denis and the son turning round at half time and saying, 'Well, he's not much cop, is he?' I didn't want that for myself, either.

You could argue that I went the wrong way about things, getting drunk and the like. But it really was all down to football. The life I led started getting to me and affecting my play. I started slowing down and defenders started catching me in possession. They had no chance before, now they started clogging me.

I couldn't take the piss any more. I mean you can hardly start taking the piss when you are three down at half time. Once, like I said, I used to get the horn at the thought of playing.

When the bad times started I couldn't bear the thought of going out on the pitch. I used to drink, so I didn't have to think about it.

Which came first? The bad times then the drinking or the drinking then the bad times? I'm still sure it was the thought of playing in a bad team, of not winning anything, of not having a chance to play in Europe that drove me to it. All right you could say that if I'd trained and lived properly United might have stood a better chance of doing well. That's true but I just couldn't see myself doing it single-handed.

The drinking got really bad. I'd kill a bottle of vodka a day, easy, and a few more besides. I'd wander from club to club at night just drinking myself silly and then I'd not go home unless I had a bird. Any bird, it didn't matter.

I used to tour the streets in my car looking for crumpet to take back to the house with me just for company. Then it had to be two birds, or sisters, or mother and daughter, or Siamese twins – anything to break the monotony and the boredom.

Sometimes I wouldn't go home. I'd sleep on the floor of an office I had in Manchester. I'd put the gas fire on and lie down in front of it and fall asleep. Then when I woke up my head would be throbbing with the fumes and I'd feel like death.

The drinking was unbelievable. We used to have a game called Jacks. There's be a group of us round a table in a pub and we'd have a pack of cards. The first geezer to draw a jack had to invent a drink. It could be anything at all, straight or a mixture, and in any quantity. The guy who drew the second jack had to taste it, then the poor sod who drew the third jack had to drink it.

I've drunk some poisonous mixtures like vodka, rum, scotch, gin and brandy in the same glass. A pint of it. Then I've gone to the loo, stuck my fingers down my throat and gone back and started again. I could really drink a bit in those days. Some guys used to pass out.

One guy went stiff one day, we thought he'd bloody died.

Another guy came up with his wife on honeymoon staying at the pub where we were drinking. He joined in with us but he was no good at it. He used to pass out and then I'd go and fuck his bird all afternoon.

After five days he came and shook hands with me and said how much he'd enjoyed it.

I said it had been a pleasure.

I was playing all the time too. The drinking, the real drinking like I'm talking about, started in 1970 or thereabouts and all the time I'm playing. My mates, you know the ones people rubbish who are supposed to lead me astray, used to pray with me to stop drinking.

They used to come round to the house and offer to sit with me, to stay with me like a fucking babysitter, to stop me going out. But I wouldn't listen. I had a fight with a couple of them. I was literally crazy with drink. The funny thing was, or is, I can stop when I want. In those days I didn't want.

I used to go for training pissed as a fart. Ten in the morning and I'd be drunk. Paddy Crerand used to say, 'You smell like a brewery', and he'd have a right go at me. But it didn't make any difference.

It was the same when I went on holiday. I once drank eight bottles of champagne on a beach in Spain, then went on drinking through the night. I woke up next morning in bed with a bird I'd never seen before. No idea how I got there.

I once got knocked off by the Spanish police. I get out of the car and I have to lean against it I'm so pissed. There are two policemen and one starts babbling into the radio. All of a sudden there's a posse of squad cars come screaming up.

I thought they'd sent for reinforcements. In fact he's recognized me, told his gaffer and the whole bloody police station has come to have a look.

The police chief lined his men up and I shook hands with all of them and they gave me a big kiss on both cheeks and sent me on my way in a taxi.

CHAPTER 11

Spending his retirement in Spain George Best soon discovered that it was almost as difficult being an ex-footballer as it had been when he was a player. He was constantly reminded of his responsibilities, or what people imagined the responsibilities were.

While Ken Stanley pointed out the commercial deals that would be in jeopardy if Best continued his retirement Manchester United, through various intermediaries, let it be known that they were prepared to forgive and forget.

At the end of four months in the sun George Best sniffed the coming season and decided to try and pick up his career where he left off. He contacted Frank O'Farrell from Spain and said he was prepared to talk. O'Farrell met him, decided to suspend him for two weeks and ordered him to go and live with Pat Crerand.

The suspension was for a breach of contract in that Best had not submitted the article announcing his retirement to the club for its approval.

Mrs Crerand prepared the spare room for her new lodger but he only spent one night there. Best regarded any club ruling about where he should lay his head as pure newspaper fodder and privately held such strictures in deep contempt.

The club sent him to a psychiatrist for a report. He doesn't know what conclusion the psychiatrist came to but he didn't rate the psychiatrist.

'He sat there with his bloody glasses on the end of his nose and started asking me the same bloody silly twenty questions the press had been asking me for the past five year', Best recalled. 'At some point I thought this is madness. I'm sitting here being interviewed at great cost by some prick who's going to tell the club what they already know, that I'm as daft as a brush. And I started laughing. Just burst out laughing in the middle of the interview. He looked at me in a funny way and then jotted something down. Later on I got mad. They sent me to a headshrinker because they thought I was mentally sick. Fucking sauce!'

The club might have been better employed sending Best's team mates for psychiatric treatment for they, with every justification, were confused by Best's contradictory behaviour and the club's attitude to him which they regarded as paternal to say the least.

Best was still popular with the majority of the players who found it difficult to dislike him no matter how badly he behaved, but there can be no doubt that the aura of disenchantment that had clung to him since 'retirement' affected the morale of the dressing room.

One or two of the senior players, particularly Bobby Charlton, made no secret of the fact that they thought Best had behaved in a thoroughly unprofessional manner and that the club would be better off without him.

The concealed enmity between Best and Charlton became public in September 1972 when Best pulled out of Charlton's testimonial match at the last moment and spent the night drinking in a Manchester public house.

The insult was calculated but counter-productive because it simply hardened opinion against Best and drove him further away from his ambition – fulfilment as an athlete.

The United dressing room became as cheerful as a catacomb as the team slid down the League table. Busby remained a grey eminence, not interfering but ever present, O'Farrell became increasingly remote from the players, a situation later described perfectly by Denis Law when he said, 'He came and went a stranger'.

Best's own form was a cruel parody of his real self. Inferior players whom he had once contemptuously destroyed took understandable delight in paying him back in kind. The extraordinary acceleration that made him a blur and frustrated those defenders who moved in to kick him disappeared and he became as easy to mark as a lamp-post.

The marvellous balance, the insatiable appetite for the game, the physical commitment and the imagination that made him so special were memories stirred only now and again as he revealed an odd flash of what once had been.

Georgie Porgie

'Those were the days – I enjoyed every moment on a football field and I discovered women': Carolyn Moore and two other discoveries: 'Birds kept me sane,' declared Best

Opposite: Sinead Cusack: 'One of the few I really liked'

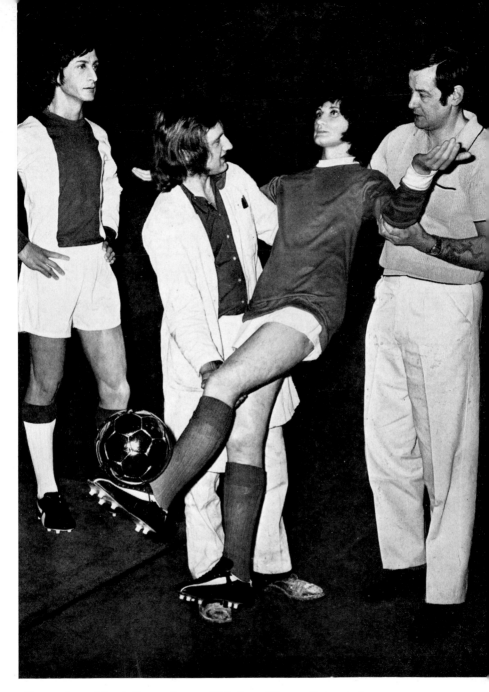

Above : Out of football – and out of Madame Tussaud's, to make
way for Cruyff

Opposite : First meeting with Marjorie Wallace: 'Not exactly a
meeting of minds . . .'

Top left: After announcing his first retirement, George left for Canada: 'I might never come back' he said

Middle left: Another comeback: Best leaves the Parkinson residence en route for Dunstable Town Football Club

Left: After the Marjorie Wallace court case, George Best drives away a free man and 'without a stain on his character' to quote the presiding magistrate

Above: 'Home from home': getting away from it all in Marbella

Top : A 'rather paunchy' George Best comes back to help Dunstable Town to victory over a Manchester United team

Above left: A beer with the lads after playing for Dunstable: 'Drink was never my problem'

Above right : Behind the bar at his club, 'Slack Alice': 'I thought I'd rather own one than pay for my drinks over the bar'

'Sometimes I sit and think where it really all went wrong . . .'

In October United seemed candidates for relegation and Best, not showing a great deal of tact, made it known that if it happened he for one would not play in the second division. Soon after he revealed yet another aspect of his urge for self-destruction by getting involved in a brawl with a girl in a nightclub.

The girl taunted him, calling him an Irish navvy, a big-headed bastard and an animal. Then she slapped his face and when she tried to hit him again Best retaliated and struck her a blow which broke her nose.

Best was found guilt of assault, but given a conditional discharge on payment of £100 damages and costs. Soon after being summoned by the police he failed to turn up for training and on 6 December after a meeting of the Board Best was suspended and placed on the transfer list.

O'Farrell told the press, 'We had to consider so many things, the future and morale of the club and the discipline of the players. I have tried all the time I have been here to support Best. It is very disappointing he did not respond to advice. He is a great player but he has not behaved like a top-class professional should.'

The news met with widespread approval. The bar-room pundits who had talked of nothing else for a year or more, the papers that had reported his every move, took the attitude that Manchester United in particular and soccer in general would be better off without him.

Neither statement bore close analysis.

He was still the game's most saleable commodity and as for United being better off without him you could argue that the damage had already been done.

A few journalists tried to give a balanced view of the situation, notably David Lacey of *The Guardian*. The day after the announcement that Best was up for sale he wrote:

'When all his problems, both on and off the field, are weighed against him Best still has been good for Old Trafford in particular and football in general. A sportswriter has professed twice this week that he finds Best a bore and the Secretary of the Football League has been quoted as saying that he is fed up with hearing about him. One can only point out that there are many thousands of people who, for a brief while on a Saturday afternoon or weekday evening, have become less bored and less fed up through watching Best play and it is a fair assumption that if ever he leaves Manchester United his next club can expect a dramatic rise in their gate receipts.'

None the less it would be an exaggeration to say that clubs fell over themselves to buy Best. As Joe Mercer, Coventry's manager, said at the time, 'It's bad enough inheriting that problem. Who wants to pay £300000 for it?'

Third Division Bournemouth made enquiries, so did a Canadian club.

Jimmy Savile, an ageing disc jockey with a well-developed nose for publicity, offered Best a job as a disc jockey and a Norwegian seventh division soccer club offered United £190 plus 'a number of superb hand-picked girls' for George as a transfer fee.

Nobody loved George. The clothing firm that had bought his name, painted it out at the Manchester shop. George Best's Edwardia became Tramps.

Stylo, the football boot manufacturers, announced that Kevin Keegan would replace Best as their 1973 star name.

Incredibly in spite of Best's behaviour and ignoring the fact that he was suspended and on the transfer list a further attempt was made to persuade Best to mend his ways and continue playing for United. Louis Edwards, the chairman of the Board, and Sir Matt Busby saw Best on 14 December at Edwards' office.

Later Edwards said, 'I have seen Best and discussed recent happenings. He says he only wants to play for Manchester United. I have spoken to the directors and to the manager, Frank O'Farrell, and Best will start training as soon as possible.' Asked if this meant that Best was taken off the transfer list Edwards said, 'I suppose so'.

Rumours that Edwards and Busby had acted against the wishes of some members of the Board and, by their handling of the affair had made Frank O'Farrell's position untenable, deepened the sense of gloom and crisis at the club. Although he had taken no part in proceedings leading to his reinstatement Best found himself the target for blame. Frank McGhee in the *Daily Mirror* wrote:

Once upon a time a first division footballer stripped and then ridiculed what should have been the love of his life – a game called football.

Then this busy, busy little boy went off to complete in his newspaper column the job of convincing young kids who idolize him that his is an example to follow.

In his newspaper column he revealed that he was fond of booze and birds. He revealed that he despised the club, didn't care for his team mates and wasn't worried if he never scored another goal, or won another medal.

He managed somehow to create the impression that he wanted to get away.

But when London clubs – all run by unimaginative fools – did not immediately form a queue to pay a fortune for him, and to him, he said he was sorry.

How noble, how self-sacrificing, how decent. His club then, of course, forgave him.

They welcomed him back. 'Start training again,' they said. 'If you don't like the set up we can always change it,' they said. 'The public will soon forget,' they said.

If you don't believe this fairy story I'm sorry – but at least it might amuse you. It couldn't happen in real life that a player could behave in an outrageous fashion and still be welcomed back to his club. It just is not possible.

Two days after Mr Edwards' announcement that Best was off the transfer list, United lost 5—0 at Crystal Palace and were bottom of the first division. The following week United directors met again and in the most explosive announcement in the history of British football sacked both O'Farrell and George Best.

Writing of the event later Sir Matt Busby said: 'The second division was staring us in the face. The team had lost all fight. There were observations by a number of senior players that there did not seem to be a close enough relationship between manager and players. Frank O'Farrell was brought into the club to manage players. It seemed as if he wanted to manage the Board too. But the fact is this, all the time he was at Old Trafford Frank O'Farrell never had anything but the wholehearted support of his directors.

'Eventually, after the 5—0 defeat at Crystal Palace's ground, the Board decided unanimously that Frank O'Farrell must go. But they also decided that the contract would be honoured in full – and he had probably the biggest salary of any manager in English football.'

In the event O'Farrell kept his counsel and made a quiet and dignified retreat from Old Trafford, any resentment he might have felt no doubt soothed by the prospect of a redundancy payment in excess of £30000. In contrast George Best went out with a flourish. He sent a letter to the meeting announcing his resignation. The letter said:

Dear Sirs, I had thought seriously of coming personally and asking for a chance to speak to the board meeting, but once again I am afraid when it comes to saying things face to face I might not have been completely honest.

I am afraid through my somewhat unorthodox ways of trying to sort my own problems out I have caused Manchester United even bigger problems.

I wanted you to read this letter before the board meeting commenced so as to let you know my feelings before any decision or statements are issued following the meeting.

When I said last summer I was going to quit football, contrary to what many people said or thought, I seriously meant it, because I had lost interest in the game for various reasons.

While in Spain I received a lot of letters from both friends and well wishers, quite a few asking me to reconsider. I did so and after weeks of thinking it over I decided to give it another try. It was an even harder decision to make than the original one. I came back hoping my appetite for the game would return and even though I like to think I gave a hundred per cent in every game there was something missing. Even now I am not quite sure what.

Therefore I have decided not to play football again and this time no one will change my mind.

In conclusion I would like to wish the club the best of luck for the remainder of the season and for the future. Because even though I personally have tarnished the club's name in recent times, to me and thousands of others Manchester United still means something special.

Yours sincerely,
George Best

The letter merely anticipated the Board's decision. It issued a statement saying that George Best would never play for Manchester United again.

A waxworks in Blackpool melted down a model of Best.

Madame Tussaud's in London was more cautious, simply storing its waxwork of Best in an attic and replacing it with a figure of the Dutch player Johann Cruyff.

The George Best fan club was closed down. Thousands of fans had their £1 membership fee returned.

But not everyone thought he was finished. A film company offered £60000 to film Best's life story. He turned the offer down.

In Canada a sports promoter offered him an eight-year contract at 125000 dollars a year to be player and publicity manager of the North American Football League. The signing-on fee was to be 100000 dollars.

Best said he would go to Canada to discuss the offer.

Sir Matt Busby told the press, 'We want to get him out of our hair. We are at the end of our tether with him.'

George Best left for Canada, but he was to return, for both he and the club had yet to face the final showdown.

*　　*　　*

GEORGE'S STORY

Canada was bad news. Nothing specific but it didn't feel right. So we split and just drifted round the States. We went to California. I rate California very highly. The people are nuts, the birds had never heard of George Best but it didn't make any difference. It did my ego good to make it with girls who didn't know me from Alf Ramsey.

We drifted down to Acapulco. I just liked the name of the place. The Mexicans did know me because they are football daft so I played a few games for the waiters' team, at the hotel we were staying.

Nothing much else happened except we were invited to a wedding and the best man stood up and said to the groom, 'May your cock never grow soft'. I thought that was the best speech I had ever heard.

I thought a lot about things in America. I tried to take stock. I wondered if things might have been different if I'd have changed clubs. Perhaps if I'd have joined Spurs or Chelsea or any decent team I might have settled down. The problem was I didn't want to play for any other team. United was special and I meant what I said when I wrote as much in my letter to the board.

I know a lot of people blamed me for Frank O'Farrell's sacking but I don't believe I had anything to do with it. Frank tried his best for me, I mean he bought players like Ian Storey-Moore to try and take some of the weight off me up front.

His problem was his manner. He was somehow remote and cold. With Matt you could always imagine a situation where you might conceivably go out one night and get pissed with him. But not Frank.

He got the boot because United were bottom of the first division. The press gave me a lot of stick at the time, calling me 'The Wrecker' and the like, as if it was my fault the club was in the shit. This is what used to make me mad. There were eleven players in the club but if anything went wrong I was the one they blamed. Mind you, I gave Frank his share of problems. He'd been a long time in football but I gave him problems he'd never even heard of.

Once we went up to Scotland to play a game and I went out to a discothèque run by a guy I knew in Manchester. Anyway I'm having a drink in a private bar and he's bringing in birds by twos and threes for me to have a look to see if there is anything I fancy.

I'm not one for football groupies – I had one once, it lasted about twenty seconds – but tonight I'm not particular because we're in Scotland which is like a cemetery with street lights and you have to make your own fun there after ten at night.

So eventually I pick out a couple and back we go to this hotel where the team is staying. I head straight for the lift when this little rat-faced porter comes scuffling over and says, 'You can't take a woman to your room'. So I say, 'I'm not taking one woman, I'm taking two, so that's all right then', and I bung him a fiver.

Nothing doing. He's the worst kind of porter. You're going upstairs for some fun, he's got to stay up all night cleaning shoes so he's going to put his spoke in. Power mad.

Anyway I argue for a while and then I thought, 'Fuck it', and I just took the two birds upstairs. My room mate is in bed trying to get to sleep and when I come in with two birds he says, 'You big daft twat', and turns over to try and get some sleep. He's got no chance.

I get the birds undressed and we all jump into my bed and get to work when there's a knock on the door and this porter starts yelling, 'Get those women out of your room'. I'm yelling back, 'Piss off, you stupid sod', and we're having a right slanging match through the door.

My room mate's saying, 'Get rid of these birds, you silly bugger', and the birds are just lying there giggling.

Anyway the porter eventually storms off saying he's going for the manager and the police and the Home Guard and Christ knows what else. I don't care. I get back on the job with the two birds and all of a sudden there's a banging on the door. I thought it was the porter back again.

'Piss off,' I shouted.

The door opens and in walk two policemen, a sergeant and a constable.

So now you've got the scene.

A hotel room in Scotland with twin beds.

In one bed a professional footballer trying to get some sleep and in the other another professional footballer with two naked ladies.

At the foot of the bed fully dressed for duty two large policemen.

The young one, the constable, told the birds to get dressed.

I told them to stay put.

We argue for a while and then the sergeant speaks. 'Just because you're George Best', he says. That blew my top. I went bloody spare.

'That's what it's all about, isn't it?' I said. 'Just because I am George Best you come up here and start throwing your weight about. If it was someone else you wouldn't bother.'

'Who's he?' said the copper indicating my mate who is pretending to be asleep.

'He's my bodyguard. He protects me from women,' I said.

'The girls have two minutes to get dressed,' the sergeant said.

The birds had said nothing until then, when one says, 'If you want us to get dressed you might have the decency to leave the room,' which I thought was very ladylike for a scrubber who would drop her knickers for a couple of bob.

So the birds got dressed and the law takes them away and I'm standing in the corridor shouting after the policemen and my room mate is telling me not to be an idiot otherwise the law is going to come back and take me in.

Now I've got the raving needle. I've been through all that and I still haven't got laid. So I pick the phone up and ask for the hall porter. When he comes on the line I say, 'You rotten bugger. I'm up here and I haven't got laid because you've called the law and if I see you tomorrow I'm going to smash your head in.'

Then I get a phone call from Frank O'Farrell's assistant, Malcolm Musgrove. The law have been to see him about the incident and what is more they have found two more naked birds running around the hotel trying to find my room. The whole hotel is in an uproar.

Next day I get called in front of Frank O'Farrell. Now one thing I could never stand is being told off because I had a bird in my room. Why shouldn't I? I was single, free, young, randy and what's more natural than to want to have a bird? But Frank didn't tackle me about that. He was upset about me threatening the porter. The porter was called in and he gave a report on what had happened to Frank. It was just like a court with Frank the judge.

So at the end Frank said to me, 'I think you should apologize'. So I swallowed my pride, looked at the geezer and said, 'I am very sorry that I threatened you.'

Do you know what he said? He said, 'I don't accept your apology.'

So I said, 'You can please your bloody self and if I get hold of you I'll knock your sodding head off.'

Frank smoothed it all out. But I think that kind of incident upset him.

He'd have had a heart attack if ever he'd have come on holiday with me. I used to go to Majorca and Spain because all the Scandinavian crumpet went there and I am very partial to Scandinavian crumpet, it being generally beautiful, always willing and a bit thick so you don't have to waste time with the conversation.

Anyway I'm in Majorca at this discothèque and it was during the time when I was bored with women unless they were an impossible challenge. If I saw a bird and enquired about her and they said, 'No way. Impossible', then that is what I needed as a challenge.

This night I am going to tell you about I am watching a very beautiful Scandinavian girl who is with a very rich American guy. I asked the disco owner about her and he told me she is a Danish princess and very cool.

I ask him for the form and he says she is engaged to the American, has been so for four years and that it is impossible to pull. That is all I need. So I move in and start talking to her and it is quite obvious she is fed up with the American and he is not too friendly towards me.

So, while he's gone to the toilet I ask her to come to my villa for coffee and she said she'd try but she'd see me outside.

So I went and got the Fiat that I'd hired and I'm waiting outside with the engine running when she comes out with the boy friend and they start arguing. Suddenly he whacks her straight across the face. This is my chance to play Sir Galahad. I walk across to them and say to the American, 'That wasn't very nice what you just did'.

He looks me up and down and he knows he's got no chance and he knows that I know that too. So he says, 'You're to blame asking her back to the villa'.

'Listen,' I said, 'I only asked her back for coffee. If you want some you can come too but I must insist the lady travels in my car because I don't want her thumped again while I'm around.'

He says he'll go and get his car and follow me. I asked him where his car was parked and he said about a quarter of a mile down the road, so I said I'd wait. Soon as he starts off down the road I jump into my motor with the princess and we are away to my villa and the boy friend is stranded.

When I get to the villa my problems begin. She goes to the bedroom without any coaxing and sits on the edge of my bed, but then starts asking me questions. Who am I? So I tell her I'm a footballer, and she starts laughing. She says I'm too small and puny to be a footballer. I get the needle at this but I swallow it because I aim to get the last laugh.

All right, I say, I'm not a footballer. I own a couple of boutiques in Manchester. She said I was too young to be in business and anyway if I was a boutique owner why did I have a little scruffy Fiat car. So I said I had an E-type that was being shipped, which was true, and I'd once owned a Rolls and she started laughing and calling me a liar.

Now she wasn't pulling my leg because the Scandinavians are too dim to go in for leg pulling. She's being serious and she is getting me mad. So she said, 'You don't own a good car because you are broke, you have no money'.

So I went to this drawer which is stuffed full of pesetas and sterling and travellers cheques and pick up handfuls and hurl it around the room. All the time she is watching me very coolly and smiling. I begin not to like her at all. So I thought I wouldn't waste much time with preliminaries. I'd get straight to the point. I said, 'I suppose a quick fuck is out of the question?'

She just laughed. Didn't want to know. So I asked her if she'd like a coffee and she said yes so I went downstairs to make it locking the bedroom door behind me so she couldn't get out.

While I'm downstairs I hear a noise from the bedroom so I rush up the stairs and she's gone.

What's happened is she's climbed over the balcony and down the pillar and run towards the main road. Now I have got nothing on but a pair of Y fronts, furthermore it is about a fifteen-foot drop from the balcony to the drive below which is made of very sharp granite chips. But I don't think about any of this because I am so mad.

I run for the window, jump through it and race barefoot over the granite chips.

I chased my princess to the main road but she's gone off in a taxi, and I'm standing there my feet cut to ribbons, bleeding like a stuck pig with only my underpants on.

At that time I was worth about £300000 on the transfer market. Each foot is worth £150000 and here I am cutting them to pieces chasing after crumpet. I bathed them in whisky for three weeks and I often wonder what Frank O'Farrell would have said had he known.

When Frank got the boot and I did too I went first to America, like I said, and then I went to Spain. I was out of condition then, fat and drinking a lot. One day I felt a pain in my leg. I thought it was a strain. Then it got worse so I went to a Spanish doctor and he gave me some ointment. But it started swelling and I knew there was something wrong. So I got the first plane home to Manchester, went to see my doctor and he rushed me into hospital.

He diagnosed a blood clot in my right calf and told me had I not come home it could have been fatal. He also said I needed a complete and absolute rest. I was only twenty-seven but I had punished my body too much. He said I had been burning the candle at both ends.

He didn't know the half of it.

The way I had been going on for the past two years would have given a prize bull a heart attack.

CHAPTER 12

The curtains didn't quite meet in the middle and the sunlight illuminated the room. The young man in the bed opened his eyes and went through his morning routine. First check the wallpaper. If you recognize it you're at home, if not you are playing away and the question is where? This time it is familiar. Home sweet home. Next, check contents of bed. He turned over slowly so that the girl next to him didn't wake up as he inspected her face. They always looked different in the morning. At least that's what he had been told. He didn't know because he never remembered what they looked like the night before. This one was young, slim, long blonde hair, nice pointed tits. Not a bad choice when pissed.

What happened?

Can't remember.

Not a bloody clue. She wakes up, looks at him for a minute, smiles. Nice teeth. 'Good morning, George.'

What's her bloody name?

'Good morning, love,' he says.

They all react to 'love'.

Next stage of routine.

Get rid.

'Well, love, I've got to go now because I've got training in an hour.'

'All right. Will I see you again?'

'Sure, give me a ring.'

'You must have thousands of girl friends.'

'Millions.'

'I hope you don't think I just sleep with any guy.'

'Certainly not.'

'I hope that you don't think I slept with you just because you are George Best.'

'Never crossed my mind.'

'In fact I didn't know who you were till my mate told me.'

'Of course. Do you have a car?'

'You know I haven't got one. You drove me here.'

'I'll get a cab.'

'It was great last night, wasn't it?'

'Great.'

He wished he could remember. He rang a cab and returned as the girl dressed. Good figure. He really did wish he could remember. The cab came and she left. The driver gave him a leer as he kissed her good-bye on his doorstep.

'On my account,' said George.

'As usual,' said the driver.

He went back indoors and contemplated what to do. He didn't feel like training, he never did. Not recently anyhow. There was a time when he couldn't get enough of it, training, that is, but now it was getting more and more difficult to turn in. He rang one of his mates.

'Tell the club I can't make training today. Tell them I've got a cold,' he said.

He went back to bed where he could still smell the girl. Wished he could remember what she had been like. And what was her name? Christ, he never did find out and so when she rang he wouldn't know who it was. She'd say, 'It's Anne here', or some such name and he'd say, 'Are you the one with the long blonde hair and pointed tits?'

Messages.

Who'd phoned while he was out? He switched on the ansaphone. Two obscene calls, a message from his agent, his mum phoned and an interesting call from a party in London which he hadn't been able to get to. They'd rung him up and all the guests had recorded a message. 'Hello, darling Georgie', said a lush feminine voice. 'Take me to bed and make love to me, Georgie boy', she said. The message ended in giggles. He switched the machine off and went to sleep.

He woke up mid-afternoon and drove to his shop in the E-type. He had a white Rolls but the kids used to scratch their initials on it. Once they slashed the tyres. He drove to his shop in the city centre where the schoolgirls, legs like sparrows, pressed their noses to the window pane and swooned when he made an appearance. So long as he stayed in the shop, so long they stood and stared.

'One day I'll throw their bloody peanuts back at them', he said.

Two Manchester urchins, raggy arsed and snotty nosed and braver than the female admirers, stuck their heads round the shop door.

'Georgie Best, Superstar
Walks like a woman
Doesn't wear a bra',

they chanted.

'Piss off,' he said without malice.

Another kid came through the door and stared at him with grave child's eyes.

'What's your second name, mister?' he asked.

'Best.'

'No, that's what you are, but what do they call you?' said the kid.

'Bloody hell,' said George Best.

He was waiting for the pubs to open. He always went to the same one, had to really, no choice. New pubs meant bother, aggravation, some joker coming up and wanting to have fight. He always went to the same pub and stood in the same corner with the same fellas. Before he went to the pub he made a phone call to a girl he'd met a week or so ago. A little darling. A bit young, but a bit special A woman answered the other end.

'Is Janice there?' he said.

'Who is it?' the woman said.

'Georgie,' he said.

'Georgie who?' she said.

'Georgie Porgie, pudding and pie, kissed the girls and made them cry,' he said.

'Don't get cheeky with me, I'm Janice's mother,' the woman said.

He knew she was, that was why he didn't tell her his name. He used to have this mental picture of some dear suburban mum, worried stiff about her beautiful daughter, getting a phone call from Georgie Best. With his reputation the mother would faint and when she woke up she'd lock her daughter in the coal shed before informing the police. That's why he said daft things on the phone when the mum asked the second name.

Back to Janice's mum.

'Sorry, missus,' he said. 'The name is George Smith.'

'How very unusual,' the woman said. 'I'll tell Janice you called.'

'Ta, missus,' he said.

That would be another girl who didn't get the message that he called. Never mind, a few drinks and then a good gamble, then a tour of the discos looking for crumpet. The night might burst into a thousand stars. The drinking is harmless really, and good fun. There's Waggy, the hairdresser, and Big Frank, the builder, and Danny, the United nut case, all mates and have been for years and when they are around there's no trouble. That comes later when they've gone home like sensible people and he remains lurching from place to place, getting drunk and losing money.

He stood at the bar all night, never moving, just steadily drinking. One day one of his mates had said, 'Have you seen my imitation of George Best?' and he just stood in a corner with a drink in his hand saying nothing.

Very funny.

When the pubs closed he went gambling. As he went into the club an elderly couple were coming out. They looked like his granny and grandad.

'Good luck, George,' said the old lady.

'How have you done, love?' he asked.

'Got clattered, that's what,' her husband said.

'Got a reet bloody clattering toneet, that's what.'

'Mug's game gambling,' said George.

'You can say that again,' said the old man.

The bouncer just inside the door must have weighed twenty stone. He had eyes like dried currants. 'Good evening, gentlemen,' he said without moving his lips.

'Can you do me a favour, George?' he said. George nodded. 'Little girl I knew fell down, broke her neck. Very sad. In hospital.

Crippled. Would appreciate a visit from you. Thinks you're smashing. Just a minute to see her. Can you go? Do her the world of good.'

'I'll try,' said George.

The man's fat face crumpled into a smile. 'I'd very much appreciate it, George. And if there's anything I can do for you . . .' He placed a hand the size of a small shovel on the footballer's shoulder.

'He doesn't hit people, he just falls on them,' said George Best.

He went to the tables and started gambling with £10 chips.

The croupier said, 'Go home. I was having a good time till you came in.'

Around him the faces of the other gamblers were elated with concern or excitement or studied nonchalance. He just looked bored.

Big Nobby, a born loser, joined him.

'Would it make any difference if I used your money?' he said.

'No bloody chance,' said George who was winning.

'I'll just stand next to you then. It might rub off,' said Nobby.

'Likely,' said George and kept on winning.

'What am I doing here when I could be home getting whipped?' said Nobby.

'Mug's game gambling,' said George softly.

'It bloody is the way I play it. Do you realize you're winning what I'm losing and we're supposed to be mates?' said Nobby.

'I don't use any system,' said George, to no one in particular.

'I've got a great new system,' said Nobby. 'I pick up all the chips and sling 'em at the croupier and say "Fuck it".'

Another gambler sidled up to George. His wife was ill and would appreciate his autograph. He signed on a pound note.

'Thanks. Sorry about your troubles at United and the rest,' the man said.

'Don't worry, I'm not,' said George.

Nobby was broke.

'Do you take Mongolian travellers cheques?' he asked the croupier, and sagged in his suit.

'I think I'll go and lie down in the road. With my luck I'd get swept up rather than run over,' he said.

George cashed his chips. He had about £600 in notes. He put them in a paper bag and carried the money away under his arm. It was past midnight and now it was time for crumpet.

He went into a discothèque and sat facing the door of the ladies' powder room. He always sat there because he had worked it out that sooner or later every girl in the club went through that particular door and he didn't want to miss a single one. Some stared back at him, openly sexual and inviting, others pretended they'd not noticed. A few came and sat down and talked to him.

One said, 'Read in the paper you missed training today.'

He nodded.

'What's the matter?' she said.

'Can't get up,' he said.

'That's not what I heard,' she said, looking hard at him to make sure he understood the sexual innuendo.

He pretended not to understand.

'What I meant was I couldn't get out of bed,' he said.

'You don't have much bloody trouble getting into bed though, do you?' the girl said.

'I'm a virgin,' said George.

'Me too, but if you are nice I'll let you see my knickers,' said the girl.

'I couldn't stand it,' he said.

He left the club after an hour and after satisfying himself there wasn't any girl there he really fancied. He tried two more discothèques but it was a bad night. Some nights you couldn't move for crumpet, other nights it was scrubbers only. Like tonight.

It was three in the morning now but he hadn't finished. With his paper bag full of money under his arm he walked to the car and drove to the outskirts of the city to a large Victorian house. He climbed the metal fire escape and knocked on a door. A peep hole appeared, an eye inspected the caller and then the door creaked open.

Inside there were potted plants, antimacassars, deep comfortable sofas and a bar. Phyllis, the owner, a handsome woman of middle age, stood at the bar. George liked Phyllis and whenever he was troubled he went to talk to her. He sat at the bar and started drinking.

'Read about you not turning up today,' said a man at the bar.

'Didn't feel like it,' said George.

'You want your bloody head testing,' said the man.

'I did have it tested. The club sent me. The guy said I was sane. That's more than can be said for some people,' said George.

'It's still daft. Who am I going to watch if you don't play for United?' he said.

'Stockport,' said George.

'I'd rather be run over by a bus,' said the man.

His friend said to George, 'Do you remember that game, I don't know who you were playing, but you got the ball in your own half past one man, then another, then another, then you juggled the ball from one foot to the other and whacked it in the corner. Do you remember?'

'I did all that?' said George incredulously.

'You did. You bloody did,' the man said.

'Leave him alone. He doesn't want to talk about bloody football,' said the first man.

'Why not, he's a bloody footballer, isn't he?' said his friend.

'Well you make bloody raincoats, but we don't talk about making bloody raincoats all the bloody time, do we?' the first man said.

'But making raincoats is not the same as playing bloody football for United,' the raincoat manufacturer said.

'I don't mind talking about soccer,' George said.

'Watch your bloody language,' said Phyllis moving in to separate George from his new friends.

She took him across the room and sat next to him on a settee.

'Fed up again?' she asked.

'Choked,' he said.

'It's a small town,' she said.

'A bloody village. Just like Peyton Place,' he said.

'Same anywhere, George love,' she said.

'I think I'll jack it in and go and live in Spain,' he said.

'You have to earn money,' she said.

'I can always earn money. Sell my bloody story to the news-papers for thousands of pounds, then sod off,' he said.

'Why don't you do what you do best of all, play football?' she said.

'Fed up with the bloody game. I'm with a bad side and I don't enjoy it,' he said.

'You can't go on like this, drinking and staying out and the like,' she said and moved off to assist the raincoat manufacturer who was having difficulty getting off his stool.

A pretty girl who had been drinking with another man at the bar came up to George.

'Take me home, George,' she said.

'What about your friend?' said George, indicating the man at the bar.

'He's not a friend, he's my husband and I'm bored by him,' she said.

'Go away. I don't feel like fighting tonight,' said George.

'He won't bother you, he's queer,' she said.

'So was Jack the Ripper,' said George.

'Ring me then,' she said.

'Sure,' he said.

'Have you got a pen and paper?'

'Don't need one. I've trained my mind specially to remember ladies' phone numbers,' he said.

She told him and went back to her husband.

'That'll be all right on a bad night,' said George.

He didn't want to go home. Not back to that bloody house. More like a goldfish bowl than a home. Training tomorrow. Must turn in tomorrow otherwise he'd be in deep trouble again. It was getting harder. Once upon a time, and not too long ago, he could go out, get drunk, get laid and turn up for training next morning fresh as a daisy. Or just about. Not now though. Nowadays getting up was a big problem, and he simply didn't want to go and train.

George Best, superstar, failed first class. He got bored during the day so he drank, he was bored in the evening so he drank some more. Then he didn't want to go home because he couldn't sleep properly so he got drunk again. Just like tonight.

A night out with George Best.

Come and get drunk with a celebrity.

A magical mystery tour round the inside of his head.

What makes George Best tick?

He'd be interested to have your theory because he really doesn't know himself.

Once there was this girl in London he was staying with. A nice kid and for a while he loved her. Then one day he just had to get out and leave her and go away. He thought about writing a note explaining and when he sat down to write it he couldn't find the words because he didn't know why he was leaving. So he just wrote 'Nobody knows me' on a piece of paper and left it on the mantelpiece when he crept out that morning while she was still asleep.

And that was the gospel truth.

He did things at times he couldn't possibly explain.

Reasons bothered him.

Like tonight. What he had just gone through, the gambling, the drinking, the daft conversations he had done every night for two years.

He was destroying himself by inches.

The only footballer who was seventy per cent proof.

He said good night to Phyllis and went outside. It was daylight. Children were on their way to school. He went to his car and two kids stopped and watched him driving away. He thought of what would happen when they got to school and told teacher, 'We saw George Best this morning'.

She'd say, 'Don't be daft. You must be imagining things.'

Little did she know.

CHAPTER 13

The joke at United was that Sir Matt Busby had a swing door fitted on the dressing room to make it easier for George Best to come and go. In spite of everything, of all the broken promises and the betrayals, Busby retained an affection for Best and nurtured a secret hope that one day he would really mend his ways and return to football.

While Best had been away in Canada and the States Manchester United had appointed a new manager, a volatile Scotsman called Tommy Docherty. Docherty's brief was clear, to prevent United being relegated to the second division for the first time since the war.

Docherty, like Sir Matt, knew that the job would be made so much easier if George Best could be persuaded back. Sir Matt paved the way with a visit to Best in hospital.

George remembers: 'I was feeling a bit low at the time. You know, nobody loves me and all that, when he walked through the door and sat down and chatted as if nothing had happened. Then when he got up to go he said, "When you coming back, lad?"

'And I thought, "You cunning old bugger".'

About the same time Docherty, writing in a Sunday paper, said, 'I want him to play again. So do Manchester United'. He then went on to say, 'I'd love to be the manager helping and guiding him. But that will never be at United because we have committed ourselves to a future without Best.'

The article said Best was for sale at about £300000 and the club would be willing to take instalments on a guarantee of his good behaviour.

While he was being talked about like a piece of furniture Best set out for a holiday in Spain. Throughout the time he was away he was informed by various intermediaries that the club would forgive and forget if he returned.

In early September 1973, with United off to a shaky start in a new season and obviously in for a grim struggle, Docherty called a press conference at Old Trafford and told a frankly incredulous gathering that Best would start training with the club.

Donald Saunders in the *Daily Telegraph* wrote:

Can we really be expected to accept that pronouncement without challenge? I ask because shortly after Mr Docherty became Manchester United's manager last December it was stated, 'George Best will never play for Manchester United again.'

Now we are told that all other players are delighted that their errant colleague will soon be back among them. If so they must be the most tolerant bunch of workers in the whole of British industry.

While they were struggling week in and week out last season to prevent a once great club sinking to the second division Best was withholding the talent that might have made their task rather easier.

In the circumstances, I should be surprised if none of them experienced the slightest touch of nausea in learning that Best told a crowded press conference, 'I have got a new set of values. The only thing that has brought me back is that I have missed the game so much.'

Frank Clough in *The Sun* was more blunt. He simply said, 'United must be daft'.

*   *   *

GEORGE'S STORY

Looking back and being honest I must admit I didn't really want to go back to football. I'd had enough, my leg hurt and I knew I couldn't get back to where I was. I don't know why I went back. I suppose I did it for Matt. The visit he paid me in hospital underlined what a great man he is and what a mate he had been to me.

I think I knew as soon as I went back to the ground for the first time that I had made an awful mistake. There used to be a special feel about that ground. I mean you could be a bloody Martian stepping out of a space ship and if it landed outside Old Trafford you would sense you were at a special spot.

Not any more though. It felt different, depressed, doomed. I'm not imagining this nor making it up later. I remember distinctly thinking, 'Oh, Christ, it's different', as I went through the door on my comeback.

The lads were great, all of them seemed delighted to see me back, all except Willy Morgan. Willy always fancied himself as taking over from me and I think he was a bit choked to see me back. He didn't like the competition and he knew that if he played to be a hundred he'd never be as good a player as I had been.

I told Tommy Doc I wanted gently breaking in because my leg was hurting me and I needed to lose weight so I reckoned I'd be fit to play for the first team by Christmas. No way. The team got off to a bad start and I was called up almost immediately. They rushed it. I suppose they had to but it immediately put the pressure on me when I couldn't cope with it.

All the old fears and doubts came back to me. I was in a bad team, it wasn't going to get any better. The only way we could go was down. Still I trained hard, probably harder than ever before, and I laid off the booze altogether.

Tommy Doc said to me, 'You'll have to settle for being the best player in Britain.' I knew he was right but somehow I didn't want it.

I didn't play too well in the opening games, then we went to Spurs and I felt it coming back. The timing, the balance, the old skills were all there. I was just lacking in pace. I remember coming off the field feeling chuffed like I used to when I felt I'd played a perfect game. I wasn't perfect at Spurs but I was eighty per cent there.

The next two games killed me. I got close marked and kicked and I simply thought, 'Bollocks. Why should I go through all this again?'

There were other things too, daft little things that don't seem to make sense but worried me. For instance I noticed people used to come up to me before a game and wish me well. They'd say, 'Good luck', or 'Have a good game', and the like.

Now this gave me the raving needle. They never used to do that before because they knew I was going to have a blinder, that I didn't need their good wishes. Now they felt sorry for me and that made me mad.

I started cheating in training, I started cheating on the field. I couldn't do it any more, I didn't want any part of it. Perhaps in a better team it might have been different. Perhaps a better team could have given me the chance to rest now and then, perhaps they could have taken the pressure off me on the field.

As it was I knew bloody well that even pissing about as I was now I was still United's best player and that without me they'd have no chance.

The end came when we were playing Plymouth Argyle at Old Trafford in the Cup. Before the game Tommy Doc said he wanted to see me. He was with Paddy Crerand. Doc said he was going to leave me out of the team. I said, 'Fair enough'. He rabbited on for a bit but to tell you the truth I wasn't listening. I was thinking: 'Christ, here we are playing a third division side at home and he doesn't reckon I'm good enough to be in the side'.

I watched racing on telly while the game went on outside. I didn't care whether we won or lost. At the end of the game I sat and had a drink with the lads. I waited for them all to leave because I wanted to walk out of Old Trafford by myself, I knew I was never going back.

When they left I walked round the empty stadium thinking of the good times I'd had there, then I went and stood on the pitch and looked about me hearing the crowd roar, feeling the excitement of great games.

Then I walked out.

I never turned round to have a last look and I never went back.

*　　*　　*

Manchester United suspended Best once more and placed him on the transfer list. The old familiar scenario was being repeated yet again. Tommy Docherty discovered he was simply another manager who couldn't understand George Best. Docherty wrote at the time:

George Best has flown forever as far as Manchester United are concerned. It's taken a load off my mind. Not that I regret my part in his comeback, but I've worried for five months in case something would go wrong. Finally it has and sadly Best had already done the hard part.

He'd broken the back of the training that was designed to help him to peak fitness again.

Now all the repair work is being undone as he wastes the greatest flow of natural talent there's been in modern soccer.

That's his choice. Mine was simple – all I did was give him his first and last chance to make good again. And when people let me down I wash my hands of them. He'd worked well. He came back in the afternoons, on Sundays, and responded to the generous help all the Old Trafford staff and players gave him.

He never complained about the tough training schedules. Everyone thought he was determined to make it and the players accepted him back and did their part in making him welcome.

But for some strange reason, all the kindness and consideration has been thrown back.

On reflection it was worth all the effort and time we put in. I'd never have been satisfied if I hadn't made the effort or had the chance to work with him. I'm not bitter about his walk-out, just disappointed. I had no inkling that it was on the cards, or that Best was becoming disenchanted with life again . . .

Although Best's displays over Christmas did concern me I didn't take them as signs that he was ready to take his leave.

And I'm genuinely sorry that he couldn't make the final effort just when it seemed we were succeeding.

We're better off without him and I don't mean that disrespectfully.

With Best in the side United were attractive but not as well organized. Without him we know now where we're going – and that's not into the second division.

Some weeks later Manchester United were relegated to the second division. At a dinner at which he was guest speaker and which Best attended Tommy Docherty pointed at the footballer and said: 'If he were still playing for us we wouldn't be in the position we are in now.'

The audience, with that perversity which characterizes soccer supporters, had previously given Best a standing ovation when he walked into the hall.

Tonbridge of the Southern League and Crewe Alexandra of the fourth division made enquiries about Best.

He simply wasn't interested in soccer any more.

He had two new passions in his life.

One was a nightclub in Manchester called 'Slack Alice' which Best owned along with three partners.

The other was the latest Miss World called Marjorie Wallace.

*　　*　　*

GEORGE'S STORY

GEORGE BEST: Right from the start I was sure we were going to get on marvellously.

MARJORIE WALLACE: We had a fairly stilted conversation.

GEORGE BEST: We just stood looking at each other. Then came our first kiss.

MARJORIE WALLACE: After a quick drink in my apartment we went off to some Italian restaurant.

GEORGE BEST: I felt sure we were going to get on well.

MARJORIE WALLACE: He was often lost for words and seemed to be groping for things to say.

GEORGE BEST: The whole evening had gone so well. A great giggle. I was feeling very happy.

MARJORIE WALLACE: I thought poor George you look handsome enough but once you open your mouth you're a bit of a bore.

GEORGE BEST: The next day we had a lunch date.

MARJORIE WALLACE: I spent the next two days away with friends.

GEORGE BEST: When we were indoors I threw off my jacket and standing in the middle of the room we kissed. Then Margi said, 'I'll go and make some coffee'.

MARJORIE WALLACE: At my apartment I offered George my hand and said, 'Thank you for everything. Take care going home.'

Extract from George Best's and Marjorie Wallace's personal accounts of their encounter with each other.

They tell me Marjorie Wallace scored her lovers with marks out of ten and that I got three. That being the case I want her to know that three marks is two more than I gave her.

In many ways we were made for each other. I mean I thought I was good at attracting bad publicity but she was world class.

Also she's jinxed. Every guy she meets gets screwed up because he knows her. There was that policeman in Kent who got the sack because of her. Tom Jones can hardly be overjoyed by the publicity they shared and Mrs Jones' views can only be imagined. Then Peter Revson, her 'steady' boy friend, got himself killed so I suppose I can count myself lucky that all I copped was a charge of burglary on her behalf.

I met her when she visited my club in Manchester shortly after she had won the title. She was a knock-out looking bird. Later I rang her and went to see her in town. We had a meal and a few drinks then I spent the night at her place.

In her version of the events of that weekend she says that when we got back to her flat she shook me by the hand and said, 'Good night', leaving me 'fuming' on the doorstep. Now I ask you, is that likely?

The truth is we spent the night together.

What is more she later said that I was a boring conversationalist. As if that ever came into the reckoning in our relationship. Let's face it, she wanted me because I was George Best and I wanted her because she was Miss World. It wasn't exactly a meeting of minds, it was a collision of bodies. I didn't want to talk to her, I just wanted to fuck her and I believed she wanted the same relationship with me.

It was funny being with her because I could see all that was going to happen to her. I could sense the tragedy because I could see she couldn't cope properly with being Miss World and all the terrible bullshit surrounding the title.

I used to look at her and see myself when I was very young and all the business was starting. In those days I didn't know my arse from my elbow and I made some horrible mistakes.

I could see her doing exactly the same. For instance I took her to Tramp which is a discothèque in London where you go if you want the world to know of your whereabouts. Now I don't mind being seen with her because I'm foot-loose and fancy free and in any case it doesn't do my image any harm to be seen with Miss World.

But she was different. She had a 'steady' boy friend, Peter Revson, so you'd think she'd be careful.

Not a bit of it.

When it comes to going home time John Gold, the boss of Tramp, comes up and says the press are outside the front doors and would we like to be smuggled out the back.

I thought it a good idea, but Marjorie wouldn't hear of it.

She marched out through the front door and next day there's pictures of the two of us in all the bloody papers.

Her 'steady' must have been well pleased.

But she loved it. You could tell it turned her on.

She was a funny, moody sod though. The day after we spent the night together she went quiet and finally left the flat saying she had to see some friends. Later in the afternoon a bird rang and said, 'Is Marjorie there?' and I said, 'How can she be here when she's there with you?'

I knew she'd got the girl to ring the flat to see if I was still there.

Later she rang herself to say she wasn't coming back, but I had already guessed as much. I was a bit narked with the way she was pissing me about so I nicked her diary for a bit of interesting bed-time reading and composed a little note for her. The note said:

'Dear Margie, I realize how upset you must be that I have left. How kind of you to fit me in between the rest. I must say you showed about as much affection as a scorpion with a headache. But I suppose one fuck is very much like another. Have a nice year. Yours in sport, George.'

Then I walked out and went home to Manchester.

Next thing I know, I'm arrested in my club and driven down to London by two policemen who give a very good impersonation of deaf mutes. Then I'm charged with, among other things, nicking her fur coat. I never worried about the charges because I knew I didn't take anything but I can't say I enjoyed the experience, particularly when the magistrate put me on £6000 bail. Six thousand quid bail!

It made me feel like a bloody murderer or something.

Then Marjorie got sacked by Mecca because they thought her

image was wrong for the job, and then Peter Revson got killed. I felt sorry for her because I always felt she'd been pressured into complaining to the police about me.

Anyway she never turned up for the final hearing and the magistrate said I left the court without a stain on my character.

The court sheet described me as 'George Best, club owner' and that was my job and my future. I felt niggled by all the events leading up to my court appearances. I felt I'd been framed, and, moreover, I felt the London police could have been a bit more sympathetic.

I instructed my solicitor to ask for costs against the police. This was refused by the magistrate.

A day later my club was raided.

Soon after I accepted an offer of £10000 to play three soccer matches in South Africa.

I had a great time over there, except for the press. They believed their own cuttings and were convinced I was a shit even before they had a chance to meet me.

They followed me everywhere and called me everything from a boring little man to a bad player.

But I was still box office no matter what they wrote. The first game I played for my team in South Africa was the first time 30000 people had watched a soccer game in that country. I didn't play well, I didn't play badly. I just did enough to get through without getting a leg broke.

It was funny being over there because they kept bringing up past episodes from my life and asking me to comment on them, and it was like seeing an action replay of all I'd gone through.

Often nowadays I sit and think what might have been. I wonder if it would have been different if Mum and Dad had been nearer when it all started. Would it have been different if I'd have been born in England and therefore able to get the satisfaction of playing in a World Cup? Would it have been different if I'd have been English and not Irish?

Would it have been different if I had been different in temperament and nature? I'm sure it would but it wouldn't have been such fun. I've had twelve incredible years where I've been right at the top and at the very bottom, and really I've enjoyed every moment of it. I don't think I'd want to change it at all.

A lot of people who are in my position end up topping themselves, but that will never happen to me. I'd be so frightened of missing something. It's like every time I take off in an aeroplane I think to myself, 'Supposing it crashes, I wonder what I'll be missing'.

I wonder what lies in store. I'm not frightened of dying, just angry that it means missing so many good things.

I still get the urge to play soccer. I'll always have that I guess. But I don't want to go back and be compared with what I was which is what would happen if I did return.

When you've been the greatest there's little satisfaction in being anything less.

Sometimes when I think about my life I keep remembering a scene from that film *Charlie Bubbles*. It's right at the end of the movie when Charlie, who is proper pissed off with everything, finds a balloon at the bottom of the garden and just floats away in it.

Occasionally, when I look into the future, I think that is how I'd like it to end.

Just floating away in a bloody great big balloon with red and white stripes on it.

CHAPTER 14

I first saw him when he was seventeen and frail as a stick of under-nourished rhubarb, and I watched him ripen into the finest soccer player I have ever seen and decline into a confused, unhappy young man who ultimately turned his back on his own great gifts.

The tragedy of George Best – and I believe it to be nothing short of tragic that he should seek a living in nightclubs rather than on a soccer field – is twofold. Firstly soccer needs players of Best's ability and appeal as an example of how soccer should be played.

The game is constantly in danger of being taken over by dreary theorists who reduce soccer to trench warfare when what spectators want is a cavalry charge. The future of the game, now more than ever before, is in the hands of the artists like Johann Cruyff, the young Dutchman who played so splendidly in the last World Cup.

It is his exploits that are burned in the mind, that reveal the inherent beauty of the game, that inspire spectators and coaches alike to a proper appreciation of the manner in which it should be played.

It is no slight on Cruyff to say that had George Best allowed his talents full flower he would be the monarch and Cruyff merely the heir apparent. As Derek Dougan said: 'Cruyff was manufactured on earth. Georgie Best was made in heaven.'

Any lover of the game can only feel a bitter disappointment that he is forever denied the sight of a great athlete on the field of play. But the real tragedy of George Best is that *he* himself will never know how good he might have been. He will never have the satisfaction of knowing the full extent of his great gifts, will never understand where his extraordinary imagination and remarkable athleticism in perfect accord could have taken him.

As Paddy Crerand says, 'We shouldn't rubbish the lad. First we should thank God we saw him play because we're not likely to see anything as good again. Then we should feel sorry for someone who had great gifts but somehow couldn't cope with them.'

The question most often asked about George Best is, 'What happened?' and perhaps some of what has gone before helps explain the situation. I have tried not to draw conclusions about Best because frankly I don't *know* the reasons for his downfall. One interesting fact to emerge in compiling the book is that everyone I talked to about it in the world of showbiz purported to understand Best's problem, or, at least, had sympathy with him.

Nearly everyone in soccer dismissed him as a foolish young man who had too much too soon.

This tells us something significant about Best's problem. He was the first athlete to straddle the line between showbiz and sport and the first to discover the difficulties of having a foot in both camps. He became a pop star and lived the life style and what he didn't realize until it was too late was that whereas Paul McCartney could stay up until the small hours and write a pop song about it, George Best simply found it more difficult to keep himself at the level of fitness required of a top-class athlete.

There was no one to warn him, no one to understand the problem because what happened to George Best had no precedent in British sport.

Perhaps again it might have been a different story had he played in a more successful side. He might well have coped better with his life outside the game had he felt happier with the situation at Manchester United for there is little doubt that he was profoundly distressed by the declining fortunes of the club and what he regarded as the comparatively feeble efforts of the people in charge to rectify matters.

To hold Best responsible for Manchester United's sad fall is to bring into question the way the club was run over the past few years. If the club had believed that Best was a bad influence on the team, that it would indeed be better off without him, then it held the ultimate sanction – it had the power to get rid of him.

As we have seen it sometimes went through the motions of

washing its hands of George Best without convincing anyone that it really meant it.

In the end Best's disappearances and reappearances, the club's hard-line statements followed inevitably by a soft-soap retraction took on the aspect of bad farce. Neither club nor player came out of it with any credit but I always felt that United lost more in terms of reputation and dignity than George Best.

Even now the lesson has not been learned, for while Best hires himself out by the game like some wandering minstrel, United still retain both his registration and the hope that some day he will return to play for them.

The key to the problem between George Best and Manchester United was Sir Matt Busby. I have little doubt that it was this very special relationship between the two men that led to a policy of appeasement and reconciliation when perhaps the best thing for both club and player might have been a parting of the ways.

In spite of all they have been through, all the betrayals and the disappointments, both men retain a respect and affection for each other. Neither will allow the other to be criticized in his presence. There is both bewilderment and sorrow in Sir Matt as he talks about the man he describes as the best player he has ever seen.

People often say, 'You're well rid of him, Matt. He must have given you some headaches.' But I don't think about that. I think about the unforgettable moments he gave me, when he lifted me from my seat with excitement and joy. That's what I remember. Once we were on a tour of New Zealand. George had one of those games when he looked what he was, the best player in the world. All right, the opposition wasn't much but I don't care who he had been playing that day, he would have destroyed them. He kept going through their defence and sticking them in the net. It was one of the most incredible displays I have ever seen. And every time he got the ball this New Zealander behind me said in a loud and sorrowful voice, 'Oh my God, he's got it again. What's he going to do this time?' That's what I shall remember about George, the times when he thrilled and entertained me.

I don't know what went wrong. I've tried to search my heart honestly. I don't think I could have done any more. I even offered him a place in my home, asked him to come and live with me and my family, but I don't think that would have changed things.

I think there was a basic flaw in George's make-up. It might be this self-destruction thing that people talk about. But there is something there that I didn't see in other people. Something that I sensed would ultimately destroy his career no matter what we did to help him.

It worries me that I failed with George because although I couldn't have done any more I still get a sense of failure when I think about him. He was one of the nicest boys I've ever had, you know. Good as gold at the club. Always polite, always charming, a pleasure to be with. And look what happened.

Still I wouldn't have changed a minute of it. People say, 'You must rue the day you set eyes on him'. What nonsense. Every manager goes through life looking for one great player, praying he'll find one. Just one. I was more lucky than most, I found two – Big Duncan and George. I suppose in their own ways they both died, didn't they?

As I wrote somewhere else in this book there never was a boy more made to measure for his time than George Best and, looking back at his career, it is impossible not to speculate on the part his rare fame played in his downfall. I say 'rare' advisedly to separate it from normal fame. The sort of fame Best enjoyed (or rather suffered) was the kind known only by a certain few.

It's the kind of fame which not only means instant recognition no matter where you go but it leads at worst to mob hysteria, at best to a public mauling.

People observe it and say 'the price of fame' without really knowing what they are saying. Best began by enjoying it and ended, like the Beatles, in finding it an intolerable pressure on his private life.

On his way to the top George Best observed one other peculiarity. The British public loves its stars to get there but once they are at the top it loves to knock them down. Unlike America which tends to prefer its stars to remain on pedestals the British delight in creating the monument and then blowing it up. George Best is particularly resentful of the press and the delight with which some newspapers chronicled his downfall.

Paddy Crerand, his team mate and one of his most perceptive friends, says: 'Frankly I don't know how he stood up to it all. I mean we're used to stars in Manchester. Bobby and Denis were not exactly unknown in the team when Georgie played, but they never had to go through what he went through. People nowadays talk about pressures and they don't know what they are talking about. They didn't have to put up with a quarter of what Georgie got day in day out.

'OK, he buggered it up, but what I'm saying is that it wasn't altogether his fault. We've got to take some of the blame. Society if you like, the people who expected too much of him, the hustlers who wanted to make a few quid out of him, the people who brought their sick kids to him and asked him to cure them. The girls who threw themselves at him, the players who fed off him and then rubbished him on the way down.

'Do you know what he was really? I'll tell you, a little Irish kid who had a great gift to play football. If we'd have left it at that there would not have been a problem. But we said, "Do this, sell that, model this, sign that", and when he couldn't stand it any more he ran away. He couldn't cope and who on earth could?

'But I'll tell you what the George Best story is, shall I? It's a bloody tragedy because he was the best player we'll ever be lucky enough to see.'

Today George Best at twenty-eight stands in Slack Alice's night-club dispensing drinks and small talk to a clientele which is as much attracted by his presence as it is to the ambience of the club. Along with three other partners he runs a flourishing business with plans to expand. If ever he feels the urge to go back to football he turns out for the Slack Alice five-a-side team against such opponents as the Manchester Playboy club. Alternatively he plays for teams like Dunstable on a freelance basis.

Often people – fans – come to see him and ask, 'Why this?' indicating the club. He ignores the point of the question and says, 'I thought I'd rather own one than pay for one over the bar'.

He doesn't talk much about soccer and never about what might have been. To all intents and purposes he is content, settled in the life of a businessman rather than that of an athlete. And yet occasionally the mask slips and reveals underneath the great athlete with all his natural instincts.

For instance we were sitting together watching the World Cup on television and Holland were awarded a penalty. The taker scored but was ordered to retake it because of a technical offence. As he placed the ball on the spot looking nervous the commentator said, 'Who would want to be in his shoes at this moment?'

'Oh, I would,' said George Best. 'Oh, I bloody would.'

INDEX
Compiled by F. D. Buck

Allison, Malcolm, 11
Anderson, Nurse, 13
Andrews, Eamonn, 44
Armstrong, Joe, 16
Arsenal FC, 42

Bardsley, Miss E., 66
Benfica FC, 36, 41, 44
Bergman, Richard, 53
Best, Anne Elizabeth, 7
Best, Dick, 7, 17, 66
Best, George:
    advertising work, 54, 77, 97
    asked to join Swansea FC, 19
    asked to make pop record, 37
    at eye of storm, 75
    bachelor pad, 64–8
    Benfica match, 36
    birth of, 7
    Cusack affair, 84–7
    dropped from team, 128
    fan club, 53, 109
    fan letters, 57
    film offer, 54
    financial affairs, 55
    fined, 84, 95
    finishes with football, 96, 98
    first division début, 24
    footballer of the year, 44–5
    goes to America, 115
    goes to Canada, 109
    impact on game, 25
    in America, 109–10, 116–17
    in South Africa, 133
    in Spain, 103, 108, 125
    influence on soccer, 33
    journalists and, 91–2, 96
    leaves football, 51
    nightclubs and, 75–6, 105,
        135, 139
    on transfer list, 105, 106, 128
    sails for England, 16
    self publicity and, 46
    sent off, 76
    sent to psychiatrist, 103
    signs for Manchester United,
        11
    Slack Alice's and, 139
    suspended, 75–6, 86, 103, 105,
        106, 128
    taken off transfer list, 107
    walks out, 128
    winner of 'le Ballon d'Or', 45
    women and, 48–50, 54, 67,
        69–76, 79–82, 84–7,
        88–92, 101, 110–15, 130
    works as messenger, 17
Bingham, Billy, 70
Bishop, Bob, 12, 15, 17
Blackburn Rovers FC, 40
Blanchflower, Danny, 17, 45
Boyland FC, 12
Burnley FC, 24
Burton, Richard, 66
Busby, Sir Matt, 7, 8, 9, 12, 13,
    21, 22, 30, 39, 40, 56, 74,
    75, 77, 83–7 passim, 95,
    98, 106, 110, 125, 126,
    137
    achievements, 72, 73

Busby, Sir Matt—*cont.*
Benfica match and, 37
Best's downfall and, 43
difficulties in handling Best, 46
envies Spurs, 18
gives up as manager, 78
looks forward to Best in team,
24
on Best, 35–6
on Best's game at Chelsea, 30
on Best to Press, 109
on World Cup win, 25–6
personal downfall, 93
receives complaints about Best,
47
refuses pop record offer, 37
relationship with press, 73
successor, 74
sure of Best's ability, 20

Cantwell, Noel, 41
Carey, Sir Robert, 97
Celtic FC, 18
Charlton, Bobby, 18, 28, 31, 32,
34, 45, 83, 98, 100, 104,
138
Chicken Run, the, 14
Clough, Frank, 126
Connelly, John, 28
Cooper, Tommy, 60
Coventry City FC, 41, 106
Crane, Frazer, 64
Cregagh Boys' Club, 12, 14
Crerand, Pat (Paddy), 18, 20,
28, 29, 41, 76, 98, 102,
128
Best ordered to live with, 103
charged with assault, 77
dropped from team, 83
joins Manchester United, 17
on Best, 19, 34, 35, 135, 138
Crerand, Mrs, 103
Crewe Alexandra FC, 129

Crompton, Jack, 19, 28
Cruyff, Johann, 109, 135
Crystal Palace FC, 11, 107
Curtis, Tony, 66
Cusack, Sinead, 84, 85, 86, 88,
90, 91–2

Deakin, Ethel, 65
Disney, Anthea, 77
di Stefano, 19, 41
Docherty, Tommy, 125, 126,
128, 129
Dougan, Derek, 135

Edwards, Duncan (Big Duncan),
8, 18, 21, 138
Edwards, Louis, 73, 106, 107
European Cup, 7, 8, 29, 37, 43,
73, 98
European Cup Winners Cup, 24
Eusebio, 52

FA Cup, 18, 53, 77, 83, 128
final, 21
FA Disciplinary Committee, 83
Finney, Tom, 45, 58
Fitzpatrick, John, 39
Football League Championship,
24, 43, 77, 83
Foulkes, Bill, 44, 83
Frost, David, 57
Fulham FC, 27
Fullaway, Mary, 16, 63, 68, 95

Garnett, Ernest Mudd, 77
Gerson, 28
Glanville, Brian, 33, 34
Glentoran FC, 15
Gold, John, 132
Gornik Zabrze FC, 43
Greaves, Jimmy, 18, 35
Green, Geoffrey, 36
Gregg, Harry, 19, 20